P. Reichman, E. P. Kibbie

The Greatest Hit of the Age and Almanac of a Hundred Years

P. Reichman, E. P. Kibbie

The Greatest Hit of the Age and Almanac of a Hundred Years

ISBN/EAN: 9783337334802

Printed in Europe, USA, Canada, Australia, Japan

Cover: Foto ©Lupo / pixelio.de

More available books at **www.hansebooks.com**

AND ALMANAC OF A

HUNDRED YEARS

Contains a correct calendar of every year from 1801 to
1900, also valuable information for the people.
A synopsis of important

HISTORICAL EVENTS

During the years from 1789 to 1890, and fifty pages of en-
tertaining reading matter.

Arranged by P. REICHMAN,
Assisted by E. P. KIBBIE.

PRICE, 25 CENTS.

INDEX.

INTRODUCTION.

ONE HUNDRED YEARS AGO the thirteen original states were poor and feeble colonies, with a population of scarcely three millions. These have now expanded into a mighty empire extending westward to the shores of the Pacific, and comprising on the north the Arctic regions of Alaska, while the three millions have grown into a population of sixty millions.

ONE HUNDRED YEARS AGO railways, steamboats, the telegraph and the telephone were unknown and there was little machinery of any sort; the mortar, the pestle, the saddle bags, and the tinder box were things of daily use. What a contrast with the surroundings now.

ONE HUNDRED YEARS AGO the agriculture of our country was in the most primitive condition. Farmers were ignorant of every thing like the scientific cultivation of their land; the plough, hoe, spade, harrow, fork, scythe and sickle composed almost the entire list of their implements, but year by year, labor saving machines have been produced and improved, until farm labor has been completely revolutionized in the United States, and now the science of agriculture holds its place among the most important sciences of the age.

THE MINERAL WEALTH of this country is inexhaustible. Treasures of gold, silver, copper, lead, iron, quicksilver, coal and petroleum have been and are continually being discovered in various parts of the country, but the development of the mines has really only begun, and large as their proceeds are there is little doubt that what is yet concealed in the bowels of the earth is vastly in excess of what has been revealed.

CALENDAR FOR THE YEARS 1809, 1815, 1826, 1837, 1843, 1854.

JAN.	S.	M.	T.	W.	T.	F.	S.
	1	2	3	4	5	6	7
	8	9	10	11	12	13	14
	15	16	17	18	19	20	21
	22	23	24	25	26	27	28
	29	30	31				
FEB.				1	2	3	4
	5	6	7	8	9	10	11
	12	13	14	15	16	17	18
	19	20	21	22	23	24	25
	26	27	28				
MARCH				1	2	3	4
	5	6	7	8	9	10	11
	12	13	14	15	16	17	18
	19	20	21	22	23	24	25
	26	27	28	29	30	31	
APRIL							1
	2	3	4	5	6	7	8
	9	10	11	12	13	14	15
	16	17	18	19	20	21	22
	23	24	25	26	27	28	29
	30						
MAY		1	2	3	4	5	6
	7	8	9	10	11	12	13
	14	15	16	17	18	19	20
	21	22	23	24	25	26	27
	28	29	30	31			
JUNE					1	2	3
	4	5	6	7	8	9	10
	11	12	13	14	15	16	17
	18	19	20	21	22	23	24
	25	26	27	28	29	30	

JULY	S.	M.	T.	W.	T.	F.	S.
							1
	2	3	4	5	6	7	8
	9	10	11	12	13	14	15
	16	17	18	19	20	21	22
	23	24	25	26	27	28	29
	30	31					
AUG.			1	2	3	4	5
	6	7	8	9	10	11	12
	13	14	15	16	17	18	19
	20	21	22	23	24	25	26
	27	28	29	30	31		
SEPT.						1	2
	3	4	5	6	7	8	9
	10	11	12	13	14	15	16
	17	18	19	20	21	22	23
	24	25	26	27	28	29	30
OCT.	1	2	3	4	5	6	7
	8	9	10	11	12	13	14
	15	16	17	18	19	20	21
	22	23	24	25	26	27	28
	29	30	31				
NOV.				1	2	3	4
	5	6	7	8	9	10	11
	12	13	14	15	16	17	18
	19	20	21	22	23	24	25
	26	27	28	29	30		
DEC.						1	2
	3	4	5	6	7	8	9
	10	11	12	13	14	15	16
	17	18	19	20	21	22	23
	24	25	26	27	28	29	30
	31						

CALENDAR FOR THE YEARS 1865, 1871, 1882, 1893, 1899.

JAN.	S.	M.	T.	W.	T.	F.	S.
	1	2	3	4	5	6	7
	8	9	10	11	12	13	14
	15	16	17	18	19	20	21
	22	23	24	25	26	27	28
	29	30	31				
FEB.				1	2	3	4
	5	6	7	8	9	10	11
	12	13	14	15	16	17	18
	19	20	21	22	23	24	25
	26	27	28				
MARCH				1	2	3	4
	5	6	7	8	9	10	11
	12	13	14	15	16	17	18
	19	20	21	22	23	24	25
	26	27	28	29	30	31	
APRIL							1
	2	3	4	5	6	7	8
	9	10	11	12	13	14	15
	16	17	18	19	20	21	22
	23	24	25	26	27	28	29
	30						
MAY		1	2	3	4	5	6
	7	8	9	10	11	12	13
	14	15	16	17	18	19	20
	21	22	23	24	25	26	27
	28	29	30	31			
JUNE					1	2	3
	4	5	6	7	8	9	10
	11	12	13	14	15	16	17
	18	19	20	21	22	23	24
	25	26	27	28	29	30	

JULY	S.	M.	T.	W.	T.	F.	S.
							1
	2	3	4	5	6	7	8
	9	10	11	12	13	14	15
	16	17	18	19	20	21	22
	23	24	25	26	27	28	29
	30	31					
AUG.			1	2	3	4	5
	6	7	8	9	10	11	12
	13	14	15	16	17	18	19
	20	21	22	23	24	25	26
	27	28	29	30	31		
SEPT.						1	2
	3	4	5	6	7	8	9
	10	11	12	13	14	15	16
	17	18	19	20	21	22	23
	24	25	26	27	28	29	30
OCT.	1	2	3	4	5	6	7
	8	9	10	11	12	13	14
	15	16	17	18	19	20	21
	22	23	24	25	26	27	28
	29	30	31				
NOV.				1	2	3	4
	5	6	7	8	9	10	11
	12	13	14	15	16	17	18
	19	20	21	22	23	24	25
	26	27	28	29	30		
DEC.						1	2
	3	4	5	6	7	8	9
	10	11	12	13	14	15	16
	17	18	19	20	21	22	23
	24	25	26	27	28	29	30
	31						

CALENDAR FOR THE YEARS 1810, 1821, 1827, 1838, 1849, 1855.

JAN.	S.	M.	T.	W.	T.	F.	S.
		1	2	3	4	5	6
	7	8	9	10	11	12	13
	14	15	16	17	18	19	20
	21	22	23	24	25	26	27
	28	29	30	31			
FEB.					1	2	3
	4	5	6	7	8	9	10
	11	12	13	14	15	16	17
	18	19	20	21	22	23	24
	25	26	27	28			
MARCH					1	2	3
	4	5	6	7	8	9	10
	11	12	13	14	15	16	17
	18	19	20	21	22	23	24
	25	26	27	28	29	30	31
APRIL	1	2	3	4	5	6	7
	8	9	10	11	12	13	14
	15	16	17	18	19	20	21
	22	23	24	25	26	27	28
	29	30					
MAY			1	2	3	4	5
	6	7	8	9	10	11	12
	13	14	15	16	17	18	19
	20	21	22	23	24	25	26
	27	28	29	30	31		
JUNE						1	2
	3	4	5	6	7	8	9
	10	11	12	13	14	15	16
	17	18	19	20	21	22	23
	24	25	26	27	28	29	30

JULY	S.	M.	T.	W.	T.	F.	S.
	1	2	3	4	5	6	7
	8	9	10	11	12	13	14
	15	16	17	18	19	20	21
	22	23	24	25	26	27	28
	29	30	31				
AUG.				1	2	3	4
	5	6	7	8	9	10	11
	12	13	14	15	16	17	18
	19	20	21	22	23	24	25
	26	27	28	29	30	31	
SEPT.							1
	2	3	4	5	6	7	8
	9	10	11	12	13	14	15
	16	17	18	19	20	21	22
	23	24	25	26	27	28	29
	30						
OCT.		1	2	3	4	5	6
	7	8	9	10	11	12	13
	14	15	16	17	18	19	20
	21	22	23	24	25	26	27
	28	29	30	31			
NOV.						1	2	3
	4	5	6	7	8	9	10
	11	12	13	14	15	16	17
	18	19	20	21	22	23	24
	25	26	27	28	29	30	
DEC.							1
	2	3	4	5	6	7	8
	9	10	11	12	13	14	15
	16	17	18	19	20	21	22
	23	24	25	26	27	28	29
	30	31					

CALENDAR FOR THE YEARS 1866, 1877, 1883, 1894, 1900.

JAN.	S.	M.	T.	W.	T.	F.	S.
		1	2	3	4	5	6
	7	8	9	10	11	12	13
	14	15	16	17	18	19	20
	21	22	23	24	25	26	27
	28	29	30	31			
FEB.					1	2	3
	4	5	6	7	8	9	10
	11	12	13	14	15	16	17
	18	19	20	21	22	23	24
	25	26	27	28			
MARCH					1	2	3
	4	5	6	7	8	9	10
	11	12	13	14	15	16	17
	18	19	20	21	22	23	24
	25	26	27	28	29	30	31
APRIL	1	2	3	4	5	6	7
	8	9	10	11	12	13	14
	15	16	17	18	19	20	21
	22	23	24	25	26	27	28
	29	30					
MAY			1	2	3	4	5
	6	7	8	9	10	11	12
	13	14	15	16	17	18	19
	20	21	22	23	24	25	26
	27	28	29	30	31		
JUNE						1	2
	3	4	5	6	7	8	9
	10	11	12	13	14	15	16
	17	18	19	20	21	22	23
	24	25	26	27	28	29	30

JULY	S.	M.	T.	W.	T.	F.	S.
	1	2	3	4	5	6	7
	8	9	10	11	12	13	14
	15	16	17	18	19	20	21
	22	23	24	25	26	27	28
	29	30	31				
AUG.					1	2	3	4
	5	6	7	8	9	10	11
	12	13	14	15	16	17	18
	19	20	21	22	23	24	25
	26	27	28	29	30	31	
SEPT.							1
	2	3	4	5	6	7	8
	9	10	11	12	13	14	15
	16	17	18	19	20	21	22
	23	24	25	26	27	28	29
	30						
OCT.		1	2	3	4	5	6
	7	8	9	10	11	12	13
	14	15	16	17	18	19	20
	21	22	23	24	25	26	27
	28	29	30	31			
NOV.					1	2	3
	4	5	6	7	8	9	10
	11	12	13	14	15	16	17
	18	19	20	21	22	23	24
	25	26	27	28	29	30	
DEC.							1
	2	3	4	5	6	7	8
	9	10	11	12	13	14	15
	16	17	18	19	20	21	22
	23	24	25	26	27	28	29
	30	31					

CALENDAR FOR THE YEARS 1805, 1811, 1822, 1833, 1839, 1850.

JAN.	S.	M.	T.	W.	T.	F.	S.
		1	2	3	4	5	
	6	7	8	9	10	11	12
	13	14	15	16	17	18	19
	20	21	22	23	24	25	26
	27	28	29	30	31		
FEB.						1	2
	3	4	5	6	7	8	9
	10	11	12	13	14	15	16
	17	18	19	20	21	22	23
	24	25	26	27	28		
MARCH						1	2
	3	4	5	6	7	8	9
	10	11	12	13	14	15	16
	17	18	19	20	21	22	23
	24	25	26	27	28	29	30
	31						
APRIL		1	2	3	4	5	6
	7	8	9	10	11	12	13
	14	15	16	17	18	19	20
	21	22	23	24	25	26	27
	28	29	30				
MAY				1	2	3	4
	5	6	7	8	9	10	11
	12	13	14	15	16	17	18
	19	20	21	22	23	24	25
	26	27	28	29	30	31	
JUNE							1
	2	3	4	5	6	7	8
	9	10	11	12	13	14	15
	16	17	18	19	20	21	22
	23	24	25	26	27	28	29
	30						

JULY	S.	M.	T.	W.	T.	F.	S.
		1	2	3	4	5	6
	7	8	9	10	11	12	13
	14	15	16	17	18	19	20
	21	22	23	24	25	26	27
	28	29	30	31			
AUG.					1	2	3
	4	5	6	7	8	9	10
	11	12	13	14	15	16	17
	18	19	20	21	22	23	24
	25	26	27	28	29	30	31
SEPT.	1	2	3	4	5	6	7
	8	9	10	11	12	13	14
	15	16	17	18	19	20	21
	22	23	24	25	26	27	28
	29	30					
OCT.			1	2	3	4	5
	6	7	8	9	10	11	12
	13	14	15	16	17	18	19
	20	21	22	23	24	25	26
	27	28	29	30	31		
NOV.						1	2
	3	4	5	6	7	8	9
	10	11	12	13	14	15	16
	17	18	19	20	21	22	23
	24	25	26	27	28	29	30
DEC.	1	2	3	4	5	6	7
	8	9	10	11	12	13	14
	15	16	17	18	19	20	21
	22	23	24	25	26	27	28
	29	30	31				

CALENDAR FOR THE YEARS 1861, 1867, 1878, 1889, 1895.

JAN.	S.	M.	T.	W.	T.	F.	S.
			1	2	3	4	5
	6	7	8	9	10	11	12
	13	14	15	16	17	18	19
	20	21	22	23	24	25	26
	27	28	29	30	31		
FEB.						1	2
	3	4	5	6	7	8	9
	10	11	12	13	14	15	16
	17	18	19	20	21	22	23
	24	25	26	27	28		
MARCH						1	2
	3	4	5	6	7	8	9
	10	11	12	13	14	15	16
	17	18	19	20	21	22	23
	24	25	26	27	28	29	30
	31						
APRIL		1	2	3	4	5	6
	7	8	9	10	11	12	13
	14	15	16	17	18	19	20
	21	22	23	24	25	26	27
	28	29	30				
MAY				1	2	3	4
	5	6	7	8	9	10	11
	12	13	14	15	16	17	18
	19	20	21	22	23	24	25
	26	27	28	29	30	31	
JUNE							1
	2	3	4	5	6	7	8
	9	10	11	12	13	14	15
	16	17	18	19	20	21	22
	23	24	25	26	27	28	29
	30						

JULY	S.	M.	T.	W.	T.	F.	S.
		1	2	3	4	5	6
	7	8	9	10	11	12	13
	14	15	16	17	18	19	20
	21	22	23	24	25	26	27
	28	29	30	31			
AUG.					1	2	3
	4	5	6	7	8	9	10
	11	12	13	14	15	16	17
	18	19	20	21	22	23	24
	25	26	27	28	29	30	31
SEPT.	1	2	3	4	5	6	7
	8	9	10	11	12	13	14
	15	16	17	18	19	20	21
	22	23	24	25	26	27	28
	29	30					
OCT.			1	2	3	4	5
	6	7	8	9	10	11	12
	13	14	15	16	17	18	19
	20	21	22	23	24	25	26
	27	28	29	30	31		
NOV.						1	2
	3	4	5	6	7	8	9
	10	11	12	13	14	15	16
	17	18	19	20	21	22	23
	24	25	26	27	28	29	30
DEC.	1	2	3	4	5	6	7
	8	9	10	11	12	13	14
	15	16	17	18	19	20	21
	22	23	24	25	26	27	28
	29	30	31				

CALENDAR FOR THE YEARS 1806, 1817, 1823, 1834, 1845.

JAN.	S.	M.	T.	W.	T.	F.	S.
				1	2	3	4
	5	6	7	8	9	10	11
	12	13	14	15	16	17	18
	19	20	21	22	23	24	25
	26	27	28	29	30	31	
FEB.							1
	2	3	4	5	6	7	8
	9	10	11	12	13	14	15
	16	17	18	19	20	21	22
	23	24	25	26	27	28	
MARCH							1
	2	3	4	5	6	7	8
	9	10	11	12	13	14	15
	16	17	18	19	20	21	22
	23	24	25	26	27	28	29
	30	31					
APRIL			1	2	3	4	5
	6	7	8	9	10	11	12
	13	14	15	16	17	18	19
	20	21	22	23	24	25	26
	27	28	29	30			
MAY				1	2	3	
	4	5	6	7	8	9	10
	11	12	13	14	15	16	17
	18	19	20	21	22	23	24
	25	26	27	28	29	30	31
JUNE	1	2	3	4	5	6	7
	8	9	10	11	12	13	14
	15	16	17	18	19	20	21
	22	23	24	25	26	27	28
	29	30					

JULY	S.	M.	T.	W.	T.	F.	S.
			1	2	3	4	5
	6	7	8	9	10	11	12
	13	14	15	16	17	18	19
	20	21	22	23	24	25	26
	27	28	29	30	31		
AUG.						1	2
	3	4	5	6	7	8	9
	10	11	12	13	14	15	16
	17	18	19	20	21	22	23
	24	25	26	27	28	29	30
	31						
SEPT.		1	2	3	4	5	6
	7	8	9	10	11	12	13
	14	15	16	17	18	19	20
	21	22	23	24	25	26	27
	28	29	30				
OCT.				1	2	3	4
	5	6	7	8	9	10	11
	12	13	14	15	16	17	18
	19	20	21	22	23	24	25
	26	27	28	29	30	31	
NOV.							1
	2	3	4	5	6	7	8
	9	10	11	12	13	14	15
	16	17	18	19	20	21	22
	23	24	25	26	27	28	29
	30						
DEC.		1	2	3	4	5	6
	7	8	9	10	11	12	13
	14	15	16	17	18	19	20
	21	22	23	24	25	26	27
	28	29	30	31			

CALENDAR FOR THE YEARS 1851, 1862, 1873, 1879, 1890.

JAN.	S.	M.	T.	W.	T.	F.	S.
			1	2	3	4	
	5	6	7	8	9	10	11
	12	13	14	15	16	17	18
	19	20	21	22	23	24	25
	26	27	28	29	30	31	
FEB.							1
	2	3	4	5	6	7	8
	9	10	11	12	13	14	15
	16	17	18	19	20	21	22
	23	24	25	26	27	28	
MARCH							1
	2	3	4	5	6	7	8
	9	10	11	12	13	14	15
	16	17	18	19	20	21	22
	23	24	25	26	27	28	29
	30	31					
APRIL			1	2	3	4	5
	6	7	8	9	10	11	12
	13	14	15	16	17	18	19
	20	21	22	23	24	25	26
	27	28	29	30			
MAY					1	2	3
	4	5	6	7	8	9	10
	11	12	13	14	15	16	17
	18	19	20	21	22	23	24
	25	26	27	28	29	30	31
JUNE	1	2	3	4	5	6	7
	8	9	10	11	12	13	14
	15	16	17	18	19	20	21
	22	23	24	25	26	27	28
	29	30					

JULY	S.	M.	T.	W.	T.	F.	S.
			1	2	3	4	5
	6	7	8	9	10	11	12
	13	14	15	16	17	18	19
	20	21	22	23	24	25	26
	27	28	29	30	31		
AUG.						1	2
	3	4	5	6	7	8	9
	10	11	12	13	14	15	16
	17	18	19	20	21	22	23
	24	25	26	27	28	29	30
	31						
SEPT.		1	2	3	4	5	6
	7	8	9	10	11	12	13
	14	15	16	17	18	19	20
	21	22	23	24	25	26	27
	28	29	30				
OCT.				1	2	3	4
	5	6	7	8	9	10	11
	12	13	14	15	16	17	18
	19	20	21	22	23	24	25
	26	27	28	29	30	31	
NOV.							1
	2	3	4	5	6	7	8
	9	10	11	12	13	14	15
	16	17	18	19	20	21	22
	23	24	25	26	27	28	29
	30						
DEC.		1	2	3	4	5	6
	7	8	9	10	11	12	13
	14	15	16	17	18	19	20
	21	22	23	24	25	26	27
	28	29	30	31			

CALENDAR FOR THE YEARS 1801, 1807, 1818, 1829, 1835, 1846.

JAN.	S.	M.	T.	W.	T.	F.	S.
					1	2	3
	4	5	6	7	8	9	10
	11	12	13	14	15	16	17
	18	19	20	21	22	23	24
	25	26	27	28	29	30	31
FEB.	1	2	3	4	5	6	7
	8	9	10	11	12	13	14
	15	16	17	18	19	20	21
	22	23	24	25	26	27	28
MARCH	1	2	3	4	5	6	7
	8	9	10	11	12	13	14
	15	16	17	18	19	20	21
	22	23	24	25	26	27	28
	29	30	31				
APRIL				1	2	3	4
	5	6	7	8	9	10	11
	12	13	14	15	16	17	18
	19	20	21	22	23	24	25
	26	27	28	29	30		
MAY						1	2
	3	4	5	6	7	8	9
	10	11	12	13	14	15	16
	17	18	19	20	21	22	23
	24	25	26	27	28	29	30
	31						
JUNE		1	2	3	4	5	6
	7	8	9	10	11	12	13
	14	15	16	17	18	19	20
	21	22	23	24	25	26	27
	28	29	30				

JULY	S.	M.	T.	W.	T.	F.	S.
				1	2	3	4
	5	6	7	8	9	10	11
	12	13	14	15	16	17	18
	19	20	21	22	23	24	25
	26	27	28	29	30	31	
AUG.							1
	2	3	4	5	6	7	8
	9	10	11	12	13	14	15
	16	17	18	19	20	21	22
	23	24	25	26	27	28	29
	30	31					
SEPT.			1	2	3	4	5
	6	7	8	9	10	11	12
	13	14	15	16	17	18	19
	20	21	22	23	24	25	26
	27	28	29	30			
OCT.					1	2	3
	4	5	6	7	8	9	10
	11	12	13	14	15	16	17
	18	19	20	21	22	23	24
	25	26	27	28	29	30	31
NOV.	1	2	3	4	5	6	7
	8	9	10	11	12	13	14
	15	16	17	18	19	20	21
	22	23	24	25	26	27	28
	29	30					
DEC.			1	2	3	4	5
	6	7	8	9	10	11	12
	13	14	15	16	17	18	19
	20	21	22	23	24	25	26
	27	28	29	30	31		

CALENDAR FOR THE YEARS 1857, 1863, 1874, 1885, 1891.

JAN.	S.	M.	T.	W.	T.	F.	S.
					1	2	3
	4	5	6	7	8	9	10
	11	12	13	14	15	16	17
	18	19	20	21	22	23	24
	25	26	27	28	29	30	31
FEB.	1	2	3	4	5	6	7
	8	9	10	11	12	13	14
	15	16	17	18	19	20	21
	22	23	24	25	26	27	28
MARCH	1	2	3	4	5	6	7
	8	9	10	11	12	13	14
	15	16	17	18	19	20	21
	22	23	24	25	26	27	28
	29	30	31				
APRIL				1	2	3	4
	5	6	7	8	9	10	11
	12	13	14	15	16	17	18
	19	20	21	22	23	24	25
	26	27	28	29	30		
MAY						1	2
	3	4	5	6	7	8	9
	10	11	12	13	14	15	16
	17	18	19	20	21	22	23
	24	25	26	27	28	29	30
	31						
JUNE		1	2	3	4	5	6
	7	8	9	10	11	12	13
	14	15	16	17	18	19	20
	21	22	23	24	25	26	27
	28	29	30				

JULY	S.	M.	T.	W.	T.	F.	S.
					1	2	3	4
	5	6	7	8	9	10	11
	12	13	14	15	16	17	18
	19	20	.21	22	23	24	25
	26	27	28	29	30	31	
AUG.							1
	2	3	4	5	6	7	8
	9	10	11	12	13	14	15
	16	17	18	19	20	21	22
	23	24	25	26	27	28	29
	30	31					
SEPT.			1	2	3	4	5
	6	7	8	9	10	11	12
	13	14	15	16	17	18	19
	20	21	22	23	24	25	26
	27	28	29	30			
OCT.					1	2	3
	4	5	6	7	8	9	10
	11	12	13	14	15	16	17
	18	19	20	21	22	23	24
	25	26	27	28	29	30	31
NOV.	1	2	3	4	5	6	7
	8	9	10	11	12	13	14
	15	16	17	18	19	20	21
	22	23	24	25	26	27	28
	29	30					
DEC.			1	2	3	4	5
	6	7	8	9	10	11	12
	13	14	15	16	17	18	19
	20	21	22	23	24	25	26
	27	28	29	30	31		

CALENDAR FOR THE YEARS 1802, 1813, 1819, 1830, 1841, 1847.

JAN.	S.	M.	T.	W.	T.	F.	S.
						1	2
	3	4	5	6	7	8	9
	10	11	12	13	14	15	16
	17	18	19	20	21	22	23
	24	25	26	27	28	29	30
	31						
FEB.		1	2	3	4	5	6
	7	8	9	10	11	12	13
	14	15	16	17	18	19	20
	21	22	23	24	25	26	27
	28						
MARCH		1	2	3	4	5	6
	7	8	9	10	11	12	13
	14	15	16	17	18	19	20
	21	22	23	24	25	26	27
	28	29	30	31			
APRIL					1	2	3
	4	5	6	7	8	9	10
	11	12	13	14	15	16	17
	18	19	20	21	22	23	24
	25	26	27	28	29	30	
MAY							1
	2	3	4	5	6	7	8
	9	10	11	12	13	14	15
	16	17	18	19	20	21	22
	23	24	25	26	27	28	29
	30	31					
JUNE			1	2	3	4	5
	6	7	8	9	10	11	12
	13	14	15	16	17	18	19
	20	21	22	23	24	25	26
	27	28	29	30			

JULY	S.	M.	T.	W.	T.	F.	S.
					1	2	3
	4	5	6	7	8	9	10
	11	12	13	14	15	16	17
	18	19	20	21	22	23	24
	25	26	27	28	29	30	31
AUG.	1	2	3	4	5	6	7
	8	9	10	11	12	13	14
	15	16	17	18	19	20	21
	22	23	24	25	26	27	28
	29	30	31				
SEPT.				1	2	3	4
	5	6	7	8	9	10	11
	12	13	14	15	16	17	18
	19	20	21	22	23	24	25
	26	27	28	29	30		
OCT.						1	2
	3	4	5	6	7	8	9
	10	11	12	13	14	15	16
	17	18	19	20	21	22	23
	24	25	26	27	28	29	30
	31						
NOV.		1	2	3	4	5	6
	7	8	9	10	11	12	13
	14	15	16	17	18	19	20
	21	22	23	24	25	26	27
	28	29	30				
DEC.				1	2	3	4
	5	6	7	8	9	10	11
	12	13	14	15	16	17	18
	19	20	21	22	23	24	25
	26	27	28	29	30	31	

CALENDAR FOR THE YEARS 1858, 1869, 1875, 1886, 1897.

JAN.	S.	M.	T.	W.	T.	F.	S.
						1	2
	3	4	5	6	7	8	9
	10	11	12	13	14	15	16
	17	18	19	20	21	22	23
	24	25	26	27	28	29	30
	31						
FEB.		1	2	3	4	5	6
	7	8	9	10	11	12	13
	14	15	16	17	18	19	20
	21	22	23	24	25	26	27
	28						
MARCH		1	2	3	4	5	6
	7	8	9	10	11	12	13
	14	15	16	17	18	19	20
	21	22	23	24	25	26	27
	28	29	30	31			
APRIL					1	2	3
	4	5	6	7	8	9	10
	11	12	13	14	15	16	17
	18	19	20	21	22	23	24
	25	26	27	28	29	30	
MAY							1
	2	3	4	5	6	7	8
	9	10	11	12	13	14	15
	16	17	18	19	20	21	22
	23	24	25	26	27	28	29
	30	31					
JUNE			1	2	3	4	5
	6	7	8	9	10	11	12
	13	14	15	16	17	18	19
	20	21	22	23	24	25	26
	27	28	29	30			

JULY	S.	M.	T.	W.	T.	F.	S.
					1	2	3
	4	5	6	7	8	9	10
	11	12	13	14	15	16	17
	18	19	20	21	22	23	24
	25	26	27	28	29	30	31
AUG.	1	2	3	4	5	6	7
	8	9	10	11	12	13	14
	15	16	17	18	19	20	21
	22	23	24	25	26	27	28
	29	30	31				
SEPT.				1	2	3	4
	5	6	7	8	9	10	11
	12	13	14	15	16	17	18
	19	20	21	22	23	24	25
	26	27	28	29	30		
OCT.						1	2
	3	4	5	6	7	8	9
	10	11	12	13	14	15	16
	17	18	19	20	21	22	23
	24	25	26	27	28	29	30
	31						
NOV.		1	2	3	4	5	6
	7	8	9	10	11	12	13
	14	15	16	17	18	19	20
	21	22	23	24	25	26	27
	28	29	30				
DEC.			1	2	3	4	
	5	6	7	8	9	10	11
	12	13	14	15	16	17	18
	19	20	21	22	23	24	25
	26	27	28	29	30	31	

CALENDAR FOR THE YEARS 1803, 1814, 1825, 1831, 1842, 1853.

JAN.	S.	M.	T.	W.	T.	F.	S.
							1
	2	3	4	5	6	7	8
	9	10	11	12	13	14	15
	16	17	18	19	20	21	22
	23	24	25	26	27	28	29
	30	31					
FEB.			1	2	3	4	5
	6	7	8	9	10	11	12
	13	14	15	16	17	18	19
	20	21	22	23	24	25	26
	27	28					
MARCH			1	2	3	4	5
	6	7	8	9	10	11	12
	13	14	15	16	17	18	19
	20	21	22	23	24	25	26
	27	28	29	30	31		
APRIL						1	2
	3	4	5	6	7	8	9
	10	11	12	13	14	15	16
	17	18	19	20	21	22	23
	24	25	26	27	28	29	30
MAY	1	2	3	4	5	6	7
	8	9	10	11	12	13	14
	15	16	17	18	19	20	21
	22	23	24	25	26	27	28
	29	30	31				
JUNE				1	2	3	4
	5	6	7	8	9	10	11
	12	13	14	15	16	17	18
	19	20	21	22	23	24	25
	26	27	28	29	30		

JULY	S.	M.	T.	W.	T.	F.	S.
						1	2
	3	4	5	6	7	8	9
	10	11	12	13	14	15	16
	17	18	19	20	21	22	23
	24	25	26	27	28	29	30
	31						
AUG.			1	2	3	4	5	6
	7	8	9	10	11	12	13
	14	15	16	17	18	19	20
	21	22	23	24	25	26	27
	28	29	30	31			
SEPT.					1	2	3
	4	5	6	7	8	9	10
	11	12	13	14	15	16	17
	18	19	20	21	22	23	24
	25	26	27	28	29	30	
OCT.							1
	2	3	4	5	6	7	8
	9	10	11	12	13	14	15
	16	17	18	19	20	21	22
	23	24	25	26	27	28	29
	30	31					
NOV.			1	2	3	4	5
	6	7	8	9	10	11	12
	13	14	15	16	17	18	19
	20	21	22	23	24	25	26
	27	28	29	30			
DEC.					1	2	3
	4	5	6	7	8	9	10
	11	12	13	14	15	16	17
	18	19	20	21	22	23	24
	25	26	27	28	29	30	31

CALENDAR FOR THE YEARS 1859, 1870, 1881, 1887, 1898.

JAN.	S.	M.	T.	W.	T.	F.	S.
							1
	2	3	4	5	6	7	8
	9	10	11	12	13	14	15
	16	17	18	19	20	21	22
	23	24	25	26	27	28	29
	30	31					
FEB.			1	2	3	4	5
	6	7	8	9	10	11	12
	13	14	15	16	17	18	19
	20	21	22	23	24	25	26
	27	28					
MARCH			1	2	3	4	5
	6	7	8	9	10	11	12
	13	14	15	16	17	18	19
	20	21	22	23	24	25	26
	27	28	29	30	31		
APRIL						1	2
	3	4	5	6	7	8	9
	10	11	12	13	14	15	16
	17	18	19	20	21	22	23
	24	25	26	27	28	29	30
MAY	1	2	3	4	5	6	7
	8	9	10	11	12	13	14
	15	16	17	18	19	20	21
	22	23	24	25	26	27	28
	29	30	31				
JUNE			1	2	3	4	
	5	6	7	8	9	10	11
	12	13	14	15	16	17	18
	19	20	21	22	23	24	25
	26	27	28	29	30		

JULY	S.	M.	T.	W.	T.	F.	S.
						1	2
	3	4	5	6	7	8	9
	10	11	12	13	14	15	16
	17	18	19	20	21	22	23
	24	25	26	27	28	29	30
	31						
AUG.		1	2	3	4	5	6
	7	8	9	10	11	12	13
	14	15	16	17	18	19	20
	21	22	23	24	25	26	27
	28	29	30	31			
SEPT.					1	2	3
	4	5	6	7	8	9	10
	11	12	13	14	15	16	17
	18	19	20	21	22	23	24
	25	26	27	28	29	30	
OCT.							1
	2	3	4	5	6	7	8
	9	10	11	12	13	14	15
	16	17	18	19	20	21	22
	23	24	25	26	27	28	29
	30	31					
NOV.			1	2	3	4	5
	6	7	8	9	10	11	12
	13	14	15	16	17	18	19
	20	21	22	23	24	25	26
	27	28	29	30			
DEC.					1	2	3
	4	5	6	7	8	9	10
	11	12	13	14	15	16	17
	18	19	20	21	22	23	24
	25	26	27	28	29	30	31

CALENDAR FOR THE LEAP YEARS 1804, 1832, 1860, 1888.

JAN.	S.	M.	T.	W.	T.	F.	S.	JULY	S.	M.	T.	W.	T.	F.	S.
	1	2	3	4	5	6	7		1	2	3	4	5	6	7
	8	9	10	11	12	13	14		8	9	10	11	12	13	14
	15	16	17	18	19	20	21		15	16	17	18	19	20	21
	22	23	24	25	26	27	28		22	23	24	25	26	27	28
	29	30	31						29	30	31				
FEB.			1	2	3	4		AUG.				1	2	3	4
	5	6	7	8	9	10	11		5	6	7	8	9	10	11
	12	13	14	15	16	17	18		12	13	14	15	16	17	18
	19	20	21	22	23	24	25		19	20	21	22	23	24	25
	26	27	28	29					26	27	28	29	30	31	
MARCH					1	2	3	SEPT.							1
	4	5	6	7	8	9	10		2	3	4	5	6	7	8
	11	12	13	14	15	16	17		9	10	11	12	13	14	15
	18	19	20	21	22	23	24		16	17	18	19	20	21	22
	25	26	27	28	29	30	31		23	24	25	26	27	28	29
									30						
APRIL	1	2	3	4	5	6	7	OCT.		1	2	3	4	5	6
	8	9	10	11	12	13	14		7	8	9	10	11	12	13
	15	16	17	18	19	20	21		14	15	16	17	18	19	20
	22	23	24	25	26	27	28		21	22	23	24	25	26	27
	29	30							28	29	30	31			
MAY			1	2	3	4	5	NOV.					1	2	3
	6	7	8	9	10	11	12		4	5	6	7	8	9	10
	13	14	15	16	17	18	19		11	12	13	14	15	16	17
	20	21	22	23	24	25	26		18	19	20	21	22	23	24
	27	28	29	30	31				25	26	27	28	29	30	
JUNE						1	2	DEC.							1
	3	4	5	6	7	8	9		2	3	4	5	6	7	8
	10	11	12	13	14	15	16		9	10	11	12	13	14	15
	17	18	19	20	21	22	23		16	17	18	19	20	21	22
	24	25	26	27	28	29	30		23	24	25	26	27	28	29
									30	31					

CALENDAR FOR THE LEAP YEARS 1816, 1844, 1872.

JAN.	S.	M.	T.	W.	T.	F.	S.
		1	2	3	4	5	6
	7	8	9	10	11	12	13
	14	15	16	17	18	19	20
	21	22	23	24	25	26	27
	28	29	30	31			
FEB.					1	2	3
	4	5	6	7	8	9	10
	11	12	13	14	15	16	17
	18	19	20	21	22	23	24
	25	26	27	28	29		
MARCH						1	2
	3	4	5	6	7	8	9
	10	11	12	13	14	15	16
	17	18	19	20	21	22	23
	24	25	26	27	28	29	30
	31						
APRIL		1	2	3	4	5	6
	7	8	9	10	11	12	13
	14	15	16	17	18	19	20
	21	22	23	24	25	26	27
	28	29	30				
MAY				1	2	3	4
	5	6	7	8	9	10	11
	12	13	14	15	16	17	18
	19	20	21	22	23	24	25
	26	27	28	29	30	31	
JUNE							1
	2	3	4	5	6	7	8
	9	10	11	12	13	14	15
	16	17	18	19	20	21	22
	23	24	25	26	27	28	29
	30						

JULY	S.	M.	T.	W.	T.	F.	S.
		1	2	3	4	5	6
	7	8	9	10	11	12	13
	14	15	16	17	18	19	20
	21	22	23	24	25	26	27
	28	29	30	31			
AUG.					1	2	3
	4	5	6	7	8	9	10
	11	12	13	14	15	16	17
	18	19	20	21	22	23	24
	25	26	27	28	29	30	31
SEPT.							
	1	2	3	4	5	6	7
	8	9	10	11	12	13	14
	15	16	17	18	19	20	21
	22	23	24	25	26	27	28
	29	30					
OCT.			1	2	3	4	5
	6	7	8	9	10	11	12
	13	14	15	16	17	18	19
	20	21	22	23	24	25	26
	27	28	29	30	31		
NOV.						1	2
	3	4	5	6	7	8	9
	10	11	12	13	14	15	16
	17	18	19	20	21	22	23
	24	25	26	27	28	29	30
DEC.	1	2	3	4	5	6	7
	8	9	10	11	12	13	14
	15	16	17	18	19	20	21
	22	23	24	25	26	27	28
	29	30	31				

CALENDAR FOR THE LEAP YEARS 1828, 1856, 1884.

JAN.	S.	M.	T.	W.	T.	F.	S.
			1	2	3	4	5
	6	7	8	9	10	11	12
	13	14	15	16	17	18	19
	20	21	22	23	24	25	26
	27	28	29	30	31		
FEB.						1	2
	3	4	5	6	7	8	9
	10	11	12	13	14	15	16
	17	18	19	20	21	22	23
	24	25	26	27	28	29	
MARCH							1
	2	3	4	5	6	7	8
	9	10	11	12	13	14	15
	16	17	18	19	20	21	22
	23	24	25	26	27	28	29
	30	31					
APRIL			1	2	3	4	5
	6	7	8	9	10	11	12
	13	14	15	16	17	18	19
	20	21	22	23	24	25	26
	27	28	29	30			
MAY					1	2	3
	4	5	6	7	8	9	10
	11	12	13	14	15	16	17
	18	19	20	21	22	23	24
	25	26	27	28	29	30	31
JUNE	1	2	3	4	5	6	7
	8	9	10	11	12	13	14
	15	16	17	18	19	20	21
	22	23	24	25	26	27	28
	29	30					

JULY	S.	M.	T.	W.	T.	F.	S.
			1	2	3	4	5
	6	7	8	9	10	11	12
	13	14	15	16	17	18	19
	20	21	22	23	24	25	26
	27	28	29	30	31		
AUG.						1	2
	3	4	5	6	7	8	9
	10	11	12	13	14	15	16
	17	18	19	20	21	22	23
	24	25	26	27	28	29	30
	31						
SEPT.		1	2	3	4	5	6
	7	8	9	10	11	12	13
	14	15	16	17	18	19	20
	21	22	23	24	25	26	27
	28	29	30				
OCT.			1	2	3	4	
	5	6	7	8	9	10	11
	12	13	14	15	16	17	18
	19	20	21	22	23	24	25
	26	27	28	29	30	31	
NOV.							1
	2	3	4	5	6	7	8
	9	10	11	12	13	14	15
	16	17	18	19	20	21	22
	23	24	25	26	27	28	29
	30						
DEC.		1	2	3	4	5	6
	7	8	9	10	11	12	13
	14	15	16	17	18	19	20
	21	22	23	24	25	26	27
	28	29	30	31			

CALENDAR FOR THE LEAP YEARS 1812, 1840, 1868, 1896.

JAN.	S.	M.	T.	W.	T.	F.	S.
				1	2	3	4
	5	6	7	8	9	10	11
	12	13	14	15	16	17	18
	19	20	21	22	23	24	25
	26	27	28	29	30	31	
FEB.							1
	2	3	4	5	6	7	8
	9	10	11	12	13	14	15
	16	17	18	19	20	21	22
	23	24	25	26	27	28	29
MARCH	1	2	3	4	5	6	7
	8	9	10	11	12	13	14
	15	16	17	18	19	20	21
	22	23	24	25	26	27	28
	29	30	31				
APRIL				1	2	3	4
	5	6	7	8	9	10	11
	12	13	14	15	16	17	18
	19	20	21	22	23	24	25
	26	27	28	29	30		
MAY						1	2
	3	4	5	6	7	8	9
	10	11	12	13	14	15	16
	17	18	19	20	21	22	23
	24	25	26	27	28	29	30
	31						
JUNE		1	2	3	4	5	6
	7	8	9	10	11	12	13
	14	15	16	17	18	19	20
	21	22	23	24	25	26	27
	28	29	30				

JULY	S.	M.	T.	W.	T.	F.	S.
				1	2	3	4
	5	6	7	8	9	10	11
	12	13	14	15	16	17	18
	19	20	21	22	23	24	25
	26	27	28	29	30	31	
AUG.							1
	2	3	4	5	6	7	8
	9	10	11	12	13	14	15
	16	17	18	19	20	21	22
	23	24	25	26	27	28	29
SEPT.	30	31					
			1	2	3	4	5
	6	7	8	9	10	11	12
	13	14	15	16	17	18	19
	20	21	22	23	24	25	26
	27	28	29	30			
OCT.					1	2	3
	4	5	6	7	8	9	10
	11	12	13	14	15	16	17
	18	19	20	21	22	23	24
	25	26	27	28	29	30	31
NOV.	1	2	3	4	5	6	7
	8	9	10	11	12	13	14
	15	16	17	18	19	20	21
	22	23	24	25	26	27	28
	29	30					
DEC.			1	2	3	4	5
	6	7	8	9	10	11	12
	13	14	15	16	17	18	19
	20	21	22	23	24	25	26
	27	28	29	30	31		

CALENDAR FOR THE LEAP YEARS 1824, 1852, 1880.

JAN.	S.	M.	T.	W.	T.	F.	S.
					1	2	3
	4	5	6	7	8	9	10
	11	12	13	14	15	16	17
	18	19	20	21	22	23	24
	25	26	27	28	29	30	31
FEB.	1	2	3	4	5	6	7
	8	9	10	11	12	13	14
	15	16	17	18	19	20	21
	22	23	24	25	26	27	28
	29						
MARCH		1	2	3	4	5	6
	7	8	9	10	11	12	13
	14	15	16	17	18	19	20
	21	22	23	24	25	26	27
	28	29	30	31			
APRIL					1	2	3
	4	5	6	7	8	9	10
	11	12	13	14	15	16	17
	18	19	20	21	22	23	24
	25	26	27	28	29	30	
MAY							1
	2	3	4	5	6	7	8
	9	10	11	12	13	14	15
	16	17	18	19	20	21	22
	23	24	25	26	27	28	29
	30	31					
JUNE			1	2	3	4	5
	6	7	8	9	10	11	12
	13	14	15	16	17	18	19
	20	21	22	23	24	25	26
	27	28	29	30			

JULY	S.	M.	T.	W.	T.	F.	S.
					1	2	3
	4	5	6	7	8	9	10
	11	12	13	14	15	16	17
	18	19	20	21	22	23	24
	25	26	27	28	29	30	31
AUG.	1	2	3	4	5	6	7
	8	9	10	11	12	13	14
	15	16	17	18	19	20	21
	22	23	24	25	26	27	28
	29	30	31				
SEPT.			1	2	3	4	
	5	6	7	8	9	10	11
	12	13	14	15	16	17	18
	19	20	21	22	23	24	25
	26	27	28	29	30		
OCT.						1	2
	3	4	5	6	7	8	9
	10	11	12	13	14	15	16
	17	18	19	20	21	22	23
	24	25	26	27	28	29	30
	31						
NOV.		1	2	3	4	5	6
	7	8	9	10	11	12	13
	14	15	16	17	18	19	20
	21	22	23	24	25	26	27
	28	29	30				
DEC.			1	2	3	4	
	5	6	7	8	9	10	11
	12	13	14	15	16	17	18
	19	20	21	22	23	24	25
	26	27	28	29	30	31	

CALENDAR FOR THE LEAP YEARS 1808, 1836, 1864, 1892.

JAN.	S.	M.	T.	W.	T.	F.	S.
						1	2
	3	4	5	6	7	8	9
	10	11	12	13	14	15	16
	17	18	19	20	21	22	23
	24	25	26	27	28	29	30
	31						
FEB.		1	2	3	4	5	6
	7	8	9	10	11	12	13
	14	15	16	17	18	19	20
	21	22	23	24	25	26	27
	28	29					
MARCH			1	2	3	4	5
	6	7	8	9	10	11	12
	13	14	15	16	17	18	19
	20	21	22	23	24	25	26
	27	28	29	30	31		
APRIL						1	2
	3	4	5	6	7	8	9
	10	11	12	13	14	15	16
	17	18	19	20	21	22	23
	24	25	26	27	28	29	30
MAY	1	2	3	4	5	6	7
	8	9	10	11	12	13	14
	15	16	17	18	19	20	21
	22	23	24	25	26	27	28
	29	30	31				
JUNE			1	2	3	4	
	5	6	7	8	9	10	11
	12	13	14	15	16	17	18
	19	20	21	22	23	24	25
	26	27	28	29	30		

JULY	S.	M.	T.	W.	T.	F.	S.
						1	2
	3	4	5	6	7	8	9
	10	11	12	13	14	15	16
	17	18	19	20	21	22	23
	24	25	26	27	28	29	30
	31						
AUG.		1	2	3	4	5	6
	7	8	9	10	11	12	13
	14	15	16	17	18	19	20
	21	22	23	24	25	26	27
	28	29	30	31			
SEPT.					1	2	3
	4	5	6	7	8	9	10
	11	12	13	14	15	16	17
	18	19	20	21	22	23	24
	25	26	27	28	29	30	
OCT.							1
	2	3	4	5	6	7	8
	9	10	11	12	13	14	15
	16	17	18	19	20	21	22
	23	24	25	26	27	28	29
	30	31					
NOV.			1	2	3	4	5
	6	7	8	9	10	11	12
	13	14	15	16	17	18	19
	20	21	22	23	24	25	26
	27	28	29	30			
DEC.					1	2	3
	4	5	6	7	8	9	10
	11	12	13	14	15	16	17
	18	19	20	21	22	23	24
	25	26	27	28	29	30	31

CALENDAR FOR THE LEAP YEARS 1820, 1848, 1876.

	S.	M.	T.	W.	T.	F.	S.
JAN.							1
	2	3	4	5	6	7	8
	9	10	11	12	13	14	15
	16	17	18	19	20	21	22
	23	24	25	26	27	28	29
	30	31					
FEB.			1	2	3	4	5
	6	7	8	9	10	11	12
	13	14	15	16	17	18	19
	20	21	22	23	24	25	26
	27	28	29				
MARCH				1	2	3	4
	5	6	7	8	9	10	11
	12	13	14	15	16	17	18
	19	20	21	22	23	24	25
	26	27	28	29	30	31	
APRIL							1
	2	3	4	5	6	7	8
	9	10	11	12	13	14	15
	16	17	18	19	20	21	22
	23	24	25	26	27	28	29
	30						
MAY		1	2	3	4	5	6
	7	8	9	10	11	12	13
	14	15	16	17	18	19	20
	21	22	23	24	25	26	27
	28	29	30	31			
JUNE						1	2	3
	4	5	6	7	8	9	10
	11	12	13	14	15	16	17
	18	19	20	21	22	23	24
	25	26	27	28	29	30	

	S.	M.	T.	W.	T.	F.	S.
JULY							1
	2	3	4	5	6	7	8
	9	10	11	12	13	14	15
	16	17	18	19	20	21	22
	23	24	25	26	27	28	29
	30	31					
AUG.			1	2	3	4	5
	6	7	8	9	10	11	12
	13	14	15	16	17	18	19
	20	21	22	23	24	25	26
	27	28	29	30	31		
SEPT.						1	2
	3	4	5	6	7	8	9
	10	11	12	13	14	15	16
	17	18	19	20	21	22	23
	24	25	26	27	28	29	30
OCT.	1	2	3	4	5	6	7
	8	9	10	11	12	13	14
	15	16	17	18	19	20	21
	22	23	24	25	26	27	28
	29	30	31				
NOV.					1	2	3	4
	5	6	7	8	9	10	11
	12	13	14	15	16	17	18
	19	20	21	22	23	24	25
	26	27	28	29	30		
DEC.						1	2
	3	4	5	6	7	8	9
	10	11	12	13	14	15	16
	17	18	19	20	21	22	23
	24	25	26	27	28	29	30
	31						

DAYS OF THE WEEK.

THEIR IMPORTANCE AT THE NATAL HOUR.

SUNDAY. A child born on Sunday shall be of long life and obtain riches.

MONDAY. Weak, and of an effeminate temper which seldom brings a man to honor.

TUESDAY is more unfortunate still, though a child born on this day, may, by extraordinary vigilence, conquer the inordinate desires to which he will be subjected; still in his reckless attempts to gratify them, he will be in danger of a violent death.

The child born on WEDNESDAY will be given to a studious life and shall reap great profit therefrom.

A child born on THURSDAY shall attain 'great honor and dignity.

Whosoever is born on FRIDAY shall be of strong constitution, and perhaps addicted to the pleasures of love.

SATURDAY is another bad day, but notwithstanding, the child may come to good, though it be seldom, for most children born on this day are of a heavy, dull and dogged disposition.

> He that by the plough would thrive,
> Himself must either hold or drive;
> For age and want save while you may,
> No morning sun lasts a whole day.
> Get what you can, and what you get, hold.
> 'Tis a stone that will turn all your lead into gold;
> Therefore, be ruled by me I pray,
> Save something for a rainy day.

SICKNESS.

LUCKY AND UNLUCKY DAYS.

Whoever in the first day of any month fall sick or is attacked with any infirmity, the third day ensuing is to be feared, which, if he pass, he shall escape.

Those falling ill on the second day of any month, though they be long confined, shall yet recover.

Any illness commencing on the third day of any month will certainly terminate favorable.

Those falling sick on the fourth day will probably linger until the twenty-eighth, which, if they pass, may possibly recover.

Those taken ill on the fifth day may become very low, but will recover.

Persons falling sick on the sixth day may recover if they pass the fifth day of the ensuing month, but they will stand a poor chance of recovery.

The seventh is a lucky day, and one falling sick on this day will recover, even though having to endure great suffering.

The eighth day is an unfortunate one, and those falling ill on it will not be likely to survive.

Illness commencing on the ninth day will not usually prove fatal.

Illness commencing on the tenth day is liable to prove fatal.

The eleventh day is remarkably fortunate for those falling sick on it; they will speedily recover.

It is a bad omen to be taken sick on the twelfth day of any month, for unless you recover within two or three days you will most certainly die within the year.

Those falling sick on the thirteenth day, if they pass five days they will likely recover.

The fourteenth is a lucky day, and those taken sick on it will recover in forty-eight hours.

Those falling ill on the fifteenth day may experience long and lingering illness, which will probably prove fatal.

Those taken on the sixteenth day may escape after some weeks of illness.

Persons falling ill on the seventeenth day are almost sure to die within three weeks.

The eighteenth is a lucky day, and those falling sick on that day will undoubtedly recover.

The nineteenth the same, though the sickness may last much longer.

The twentieth is an uncertain day, and sickness commencing on this day frequently terminates fatally if it continue more than five days.

The twenty-first day perils ones life for ten days, that time passed, you will recover.

Those falling sick on the twenty-second, if they do not recover in forty-eight hours, will die.

Those taken sick on the twenty-third will stand a chance of lingering illness, which will probably terminate favorably.

The twenty-fourth is another unlucky day, and those falling ill on that day, though they be partially restored, will probably die within three months.

The twenty-fifth is a very favorable day, and those falling sick will get well speedily.

The twenty-sixth portends a protracted illness, which will terminate favorably.

The twenty-seventh threatens death, though the chances of recovery are fair.

Death threatens him or her who falls ill on the twenty-eighth.

Persons who are taken sick on the twenty-ninth day, will have a very protracted illness and recover slowly.

The thirtieth and thirty-first are uncertain days, and to persons falling sick on either of these days, it cannot be foretold whether they will recover or not.

ASTROLOGICAL MISCELLANY.

In January, six days, the 1st, 2d, 15th, 26th, 27th, 28th.
In February, four days, the 11th, 21st, 25th, 26th.
In March, two days, the 10th, 24th.
In April, five days, the 6th, 15th, 16th, 20th, 28th.
In May, three days, the 3d, 18th, 31st.
In June, five days, the 10th, 11th, 15th, 22d, 25th.
In July, three days, the 9th, 15th, 28th.
In August, six days, the 6th, 7th, 10th, 11th, 19th, 25th.
In September, five days, the 4th, 8th, 17th, 18th, 23d.
In October, five days, the 3d, 7th, 16th, 21st, 22d.
In November, three days, the 5th, 14th, 20th.
In December, six days, the 15th, 19th, 20th, 22d, 23d, 25th.

UNFORTUNATE DAYS OF THE MONTH.

In January, seven days, the 3d, 4th, 6th, 13th, 14th, 20th, 21st.

In February, seven days, the 3d, 7th, 9th, 12th, 16th, 17th, 23d.

In March, eight days, the 1st, 2d, 5th, 8th, 12th, 16th, 28th, 29th.

In April, two days, the 24th, 25th.

In May, five days, the 17th, 20th, 27th, 29th, 30th.

In June, eight days, the 1st, 5th, 6th, 9th, 12th, 16th, 18th, 24th.

In July, four days, the 3d, 10th, 17th, 18th.

In August, two days, the 15th, 20th.

In September, two days, the 9th, 16th.

In October, six days, the 4th, 9th, 11th, 17th, 27th, 31st.

In November, four days, the 3d, 9th, 10th, 21st.

In December, two days, the 14th, 21st.

PREDICTIONS OF THE WEATHER,

ATMOSPHERIC CHANGES, ETC.

Should the horizon in the north wear a ruddy appearance in the evening, stormy weather may be expected.

If the clouds in the south are ruddy in the evening, sunshiny and rainy weather will alternately prevail for some time afterward.

When the face of the moon is partially obscured by a light, thin vapor, rain will shortly follow.

When the sun's rays at mid-day are more than ordinarily dazzling, rainy weather will shortly succeed.

In summer, when the swallows fly close to the ground, rainy weather will surely soon follow.

The shrill crowing of a cock during rainy weather at mid-day or evening, is a sign of approaching dry weather.

When the smoke from the chimney falls downward instead of rising upward, rainy weather will soon follow.

If on a foggy morning in summer the fog rises upward, it will be a fine day; if the fog falls to the ground it will be wet.

When in summer time you see the cattle grazing in a field gathering together in groups, be assured that a thunder-storm is approaching.

When you see the fowls in a barnyard flocking together under some cover, be assured that unpleasant weather is near at hand.

When your dog or cat is more than ordinarily restless, frisking about the house in all directions, be assured that boisterous weather will shortly follow.

In summer, when the atmosphere is dense and heavy, and there is scarcely a breath of air, be assured that a thunder-storm is coming on.

When the rising sun appears like a solid mass of heated metal, and no rays appear to emanate therefrom, fine and dry weather may be confidently anticipated.

When the sun sets in a halo of ruddy brightness, genial and bright weather may be fully relied on for the next day.

When the moon appears of a ruddy hue, stormy and boisterous weather may be expected.

When the stars appear of a sparkling brightness, fine and genial weather may be expected to prevail for some time; should they appear obscure and dim, changeable and rainy weather may be anticipated.

When sea birds are observed flocking towards the shore, storms and tempests may be confidently expected.

When in the early autumn season the migratory birds are seen flocking together and taking their departure, it is a sure sign that rough weather is approaching, and that a severe winter may be expected.

When the doves around a dovecot make a more than ordinary cooing and frequently pass in and out of their cot, it is a sign that a change of weather is near.

When the robin approaches your dwelling, it is a sign that wintry weather is close at hand.

When there is a thick vapory mist resting on the tops of high hills in the morning and remains during the day, wet and unpleasant weather may be expected. Should the mist eventually rise upward and be evaporated by the sun's rays, a return to dry weather may be looked for; if, however, the mist falls down into the valley, a continuation of wet weather will prevail.

PHYSIOGNOMY.

STRENGH OF BODY is shown by stiff hair, large bones, firm and robust limbs, short muscular neck, firm and erect carriage, head broad and high, forehead short and peaked, large feet, harsh voice, and florid complexion.

WEAKNESS OF BODY is distinguished by a small ill proportioned head, narrow shoulders, soft skin and pale complexion.

LONG LIFE is indicated by strong teeth, sanguine temperament, middle size, large, deep and ruddy lines in the hand, large muscles, stooping shoulders, full chest, firm flesh, clear complexion, slow growth, wide ears, and large eyelids.

SHORT LIFE may be inferred from a thick tongue, the appearance of the molars before the age of puberty, thin, uneven teeth, confused lines in the hand, and quick but small growth.

INTELLECT is denoted by thin skin, middle stature, bright eyes, fair complexion, straight and fine hair, eyebrows joined, affable manner, moderation in mirth, and the temples slightly concave.

A DUNCE may be known by a swollen neck, a round head, fleshy forehead, pale dull eyes, snuffling nostrils, little hands, blubber lips, short fingers and thick legs.

FORTITUDE is promised from a wide mouth, slow, grave and always equal, open, steadfast eys, hair high above the forehead, the forehead square and high, the neck firm though not fleshy, large chest, and dark complexion.

INTREPIDITY often resides in a small body, with ruddy countenance, frowning eyebrows, small mouth, prominent nose, and large lines in the hand.

BOLDNESS is characterized by a prominent mouth, rugged appearance, rough forehead, arched eyebrows, large nostrils and teeth, short neck, strong arms, ample chest, and square shoulders.

TIMIDITY resides where we find a concave neck, pale color, weak eyes, soft hair, plump breast, shrill voice, thin lips, broad thin hands and small shambling feet.

PRUDENCE is distinguished by a head which is flat on the sides, broad square forehead, soft voice, broad chest, thin hair, bright eyes, large ears and aquiline nose.

IRASCIBILITY may be seen in an erect carriage, clear skin, solemn voice, open nostrils, thick neck, quick pace, bloodshot eyes, large and unequal teeth.

MELANCHOLY is denoted by a wrinkled face, dejected eyes, slow pace, fixed look, and deliberate respiration.

AMOROUSNESS shows a fair, slender face, hair exuberant on head, face and limbs, moist shining eyes, wide nostrils, and prominent lips.

GAIETY shows a rosy agreeable countenance, musical voice, an agile body and soft flesh.

ENVY appears with a wrinkled forehead, frowning, dejected look, pale countenance and dry, rough skin.

GENTLENESS may be distinguished by a soft and moist palm, frequent shutting of the eyes, soft movement, slow speech, and fine hair.

BASHFULNESS may be discovered by moist half closed eyes, moderate pace, slow speech, and blushing countenance.

SOBRIEY is accompanied by equal respiration, regular features, easy carriage and sedate manners.

MENTAL STRENGTH is signified by straight hair, a small body, shining eyes, grave, intense voice, broad back and shoulders.

GOOD MEMORY is common in those persons who are small, yet better formed in the upper than the lower parts, delicate skin, crooked nose, thick teeth, large ears.

BAD MEMORY is observable in persons who are larger in their superior than inferior parts, hairy hands and body, coarse skin.

GOOD SIGHT is enjoyed by those persons who have black, thick, straight eyelashes, large bushy eyebrows.

HEARING is most acute in those whose ears are well furnished with cartilage, well channeled and hairy.

SMELLING is most perfect in those who have large noses, descending very near the mouth, neither too moist nor too dry.

TASTING is dainty in such as have a spongy soft tongue, well moistened with saliva.

DELICACY OF TOUCH is remarked in those who have sensitive nerves, soft skin, moderately warm and dry.

CONCISE BUSINESS RULES.

The intelligent and upright business man regulates his conduct by fixed principles and established methods.

He is strict in keeping his engagements.

He does nothing carelessly or hurriedly.

He don't intrust to others what he can easily do himself.

He don't leave undone what should and can be done.

Frank with all, he keeps his plans and views to himself.

He is prompt and decisive in his dealings and don't over trade.

He prefers short credits to long ones, and cash to credit always.

He is clear and explicit in his bargains.

He don't leave to memory what should be in writing.

He keeps copies of all important letters sent, and files carefully all papers of value.

He don't allow his desk to be littered, but keeps it tidy and well arranged.

He keeps everything in its proper place.

He keeps the details of his business well in hand and under his own eye.

He believes that those whose credit is suspected are not to be trusted.

He often examines his books and knows how he stands.

He has certain times for balancing his books and sending out accounts that are due.

He never takes money risks that can be avoided and shuns litigation.

He is careful about expenses and keeps within his income.

He don't postpone until to-morrow what can be done to-day.

He is extremely careful about endorsing for any one.

To claims of real need he responds generously.

BRIEF BUSINESS LAWS.

1. Ignorance of law excuses no one.
2. It is a fraud to conceal a fraud.
3. The law compels no man to do impossibilities.
4. An agreement without a consideration is void.
5. Signatures made with a lead pencil are good in law.
6. A receipt for money paid is not legally conclusive.
7. The acts of one partner bind all the others.
8. Contracts made on Sunday can not be enforced.
9. A contract made with a minor is invalid.
10. A contract made with a lunatic is void.
11. Contracts for advertising in Sunday newspapers are invalid.
12. Principals are responsible for the acts of their agents.
13. Agents are responsible to their principals for errors.
14. Each individual in a partnership is responsible for the whole amount of the debt of the firm.
15. A note given by a minor is void.
16. Notes bear interest only when so worded.
17. It is not legally necessary to say on a note "for value received."
18. A note drawn on Sunday is void.
19. A note obtained by fraud or from a person in a state of intoxication can not be collected.
20. If a note be lost or stolen it does not release the maker; he must pay it.
21. The endorser of a note is exempt from liability if not served with notice of its dishonor within twenty-four hours of its non-payment.

LEGAL HOLIDAYS IN VARIOUS STATES.

January 1st, or New Year's day, is a legal holiday in all the states except Arkansas, Delaware, Georgia, Kentucky, Maine, Massachusetts, New Hampshire, Rhode Island and North and South Carolina.

February 22d, or Washington's birthday, is a legal holiday in all the states except Alabama, Florida, Arkansas, Illinois, Indiana, Iowa, Kansas, Maine, Missouri, North Carolina, Ohio, Oregon, Tennessee and Texas.

, May 30th, or Decoration day, is a legal holiday only in Colorado, Connecticut, Maine, Michigan, New Hampshire, New Jersey, New York, Rhode Island, Pennsylvania and Vermont.

January 8th, the anniversary of the battle of New Orleans, February 12th, the anniversary of the birth of Abraham Lincoln, and March 4th, the Firemen's anniversary, are legal holidays in Louisiana.

July 4th, Independence day, is a legal holiday in all the states and territories.

December 25th, Christmas day, is a legal holiday in all the states and territories.

Thanksgiving day and public fast days appointed by the president, are legal holidays. Such days are legal holidays in such states as may set them apart for religious observance by proclamation of the govenor.

Days appointed for General Elections, State or National, are legal holidays in California, Maine, Missouri, New Jersey, New York, Oregon, South Carolina and Wisconsin.

Good Friday is a legal holiday in Louisiana and in the cities of Mobile, Montgomery and Selma, Alabama.

Memorial Day, April 20th, is a legal holiday in Georgia.

March 2d, the anniversary of the Independence of Texas, and April 21st, the anniversary of the Battle of San Jacinto, are legal holidays in Texas.

CHOICE LIFE MAXIMS.

1. Affectation is at best a deformity.
2. Ask thy purse what thou shouldst buy.
3. Be slow in choosing a friend, but slower in exchanging him.
4. Before you attempt anything, consider what you can do.
5. By reading you enrich the mind, by conversation you polish it.
6. Consideration is due to all things.
7. If you would teach secrecy to others begin with yourself.
8. In order to judge of another's feelings remember your own.
9. Let your anger set with the sun, but not rise with it.
10. None have less praise than those who seek most after it.
11. Pride is as loud a beggar as want, and a great deal more saucy.
12. Rage robs a man of his reason, and makes him a laughing stock.
13. Apply the golden rule to your every act and thought.

HEALTH MAXIMS.

Don't sleep in a draught.
Don't go to bed with cold feet.
Don't stand over hot air registers.
Dod't try to cool too quickly after exercising.
Don't eat merely to save food and get your money's worth
Don't sleep with insecure false teeth in your mouth.
Don't sleep in a room without proper ventilation.
Don't stuff a cold lest you be obliged to starve a fever.
Don't neglect constipated bowels.
Don't use your voice much when very hoarse.

Don't try to get along without woolen underclothing in winter.

Don't sleep in the same undergarment you wear during the day.

Don't try to keep up on coffee and alcohol when you ought to go to bed.

Don't drink ice water rapidly ; sip it quite slowly.

Don't bring on baldness and headache by wearing close warm head covering.

Don't try to lengthen your days by cutting short your night's rest.

Don't ruin your eyes by reading or working by dim or flickering light.

Don't experiment with drugs because you fancy yourself sick.

Don't eat between meals, unless it should be ripe fruits or a glass of hot milk.

Don't imagine that stimulants will help you to bear heat or cold.

Don't eat pork or veal when you can get beef or mutton.

Don't expect to cure dyspepsia by using pastry and rich fruit cake.

Don't neglect to keep the feet warm, the head cool and the bowels open, in order to promote health.

Look to your health, and if you have it, praise God, and value it next to a good conscience, for health is the second blessing that we mortals are capable of—a blessing that money cannot buy. Value it.

Surround the sick man with the pomp of royalty, let his couch be a throne and his crutch a sceptre. He will look with con-temptuous eye on marble, on gold, on purple, and would deem himself happy could he enjoy even under a thatched roof the health of the meanest of his subjects.

ORIGIN OF FAMILIAR WORDS AND PHRASES.

ALMIGHTY DOLLAR. Washington Irving first employed the expression in his "Creole Village."

ARGUS EYED. According to Grecian fable, Juno being jealous of Io, had her constantly watched by Argus, who had a hundred eyes.

BARKING DOGS NEVER BITE. Barking is a habit acquired in a domesticated state, as dogs in a wild state never bark, but whine, growl, or howl.

BEWARE OF AFTER CLAPS. An after clap is something following after an affair is supposed to be over; in thunderstorms a clap is often heard after the rain subsides and the cloud breaks.

BILLINGSGATE. Coarse, vulgar language, like that of the Billingsgate fish woman.

BLACK MAIL. Money, corn or cattle, anciently paid in the north of England to free-booters to insure for themselves protection from pillage.

BLIND AS A BEETLE. The door Beetle, although not blind as is usually supposed, in its rapid flight blunders against any obstacle as if it could not see.

BOHEMIAN. A term attached to artists and literary men of unsettled manner of living.

BONFIRE. A fire made as an expression of public joy or for amusement.

BOOBY. A dunce, a stupid fellow.

BROTHER JONATHAN. The original was Jonathan Trumbull, governor of Connecticut, to whom Washington, when in a strait for supplies, always applied to, saying: "We must consult Brother Jonathan."

BULL. A blunder or contradiction, for which the Irish are phenomenal.

BURY THE HATCHET. Forget the past; derived from the Indians, who buried their hatchets, scalping knifes, and war clubs, to bury the thought of hostility out of sight.

CATCH A TARTAR. To be outdone. An Irish soldier in a battle against the Turks, shouted to his officer that he had caught a Tartar. "Bring him along!" said the officer. "But he won't come." "Then come along yourself!" "Arrah! and so I would but he won't let me," answered Paddy.

COME UP TO THE SCRATCH. An allusion to prize fighting, where a line is scratched on the ground, which the toe of the fighter must come up to.

DOG DAYS, from July 3 to August 11, the Romans thought that the dog star rising with the sun increased its heat, hence the dog days possessed the combined heat of the dog star and the sun.

FATHER OF HIS COUNTRY. Cicero was styled so by the Romans. Andrea Dorea by the Genoese, 1468-1560. George Washington by the Americans, 1732-1799.

A NICE BERTH. A fortunate position.

IN THE LONG RUN. In running a race one may outstrip the others at the start, but be the last in the long run.

BLOW HIM UP SKY HIGH. Give him a regular scolding; borrowed from blasting by gunpowder.

LET THE COBBLER STICK TO HIS LAST. Said by Appeles to a conceited cobbler who found fault with one of his famous paintings.

LIKE IT OR LUMP IT. If not pleased, sulk; in Devonshire "lumps" is equivalent to "sulks."

OLD SCRATCH. Satan from Schraatz a Scandinavian demon.

PAWNBROKER. The sign of three golden balls took its origin from three gilded pills, used by the Medici family in token of their profession of medicine. They were rich Florentine merchants, who lent money.

SCHOOLMASTER ABROAD. Lord Brougham once said: Let the soldier be abroad if he will, he can do nothing in this age. There is another personage abroad, it is the schoolmaster, and I trust t~ him, armed with his Primer, against the soldier in full array.

SHAKING HANDS. In ancient times when in concluding an armistice, adversaries took each other by the weapon hand as a safeguard against treachery.

SIGNING THE NAME. In olden times those who could write as well as those who could not, added the sign of the cross for its greater assurance.

TAKING OFF THE HAT. Derived from the ancient custom of removing the helmet when not in danger; hence a man lifting his hat shows that he is not afraid to remain unarmed in ones presence.

A FEATHER IN YOUR CAP. A mark of distinction. This originates with the wild tribes of Asia and America, who added a new feather to their head-dress for every enemy slain.

THAT'S A MERE BLIND. A pretence; something to conceal a real design.

THERE'S MANY A SLIP TWIXT CUP AND LIP. Ameaus, king of Samos, planted a vineyard, but was warned by a seer that he would never drink of the wine made from its grapes. Wine having been made, he was in the act of raising the cup to his lips, when he was told that a wild boar was laying waste his vineyard. He left the wine untasted and attacked the boar, but was killed and never tasted the wine; hence the proverb.

TO RECKON WITHOUT ONE'S HOST. Is to make an estimate from your own standpoint, regardless of considerations from another point of view. Guests may calculate their own bills, but the host will introduce items which they have not taken into account.

UP THE SPOUT. Pawnbrokers formerly sent articles pawned up a spout, through which they were returned when redeemed.

WITH ONE FOOT IN THE GRAVE. Very near death. Julian is reported to have said that he would learn something even if he had one foot in the grave.

DREAMS AND THEIR INTERPRETATION.

Although many differences exist as to the origination of dreams, and the various interpretations given them, the fact is incontrovertible that they have, in all ages and among all nations, borne a conspicuous part in shaping destinies. Both sacred and profane history is replete with dreams which have had more or less influence upon the lives of the dreamers Innumerable are the instances in which have been prefigured in dreams, occurences that have actually taken place, and many dangers have been averted by heeding warnings given during sleep. Of course, it would be unwise to place full credence in the prognostications of all dreams and equally so to totally disregard them. To both the educated and the illiterate, dreams of whatever nature, point a moral, and those who heedlessly ignore their lessons often experience cause for regret. In the following pages will be found a complete collection of the scientific and philosophic researches of many gifted in the art of divination.

ACQUAINTANCE, to fight with them, distraction. ADVERSARY, a speedy dispatch of your business. ALMONDS, difficulties. ALMS, to give, joy and gladness; to refuse, want and misery. ANCHOR, certain joys, assurance. ALTAR, joy. ANGEL, a good omen. ANGER, powerful enemies. ANGLING, affliction and trouble. APES, enemies, deceit. ASSES, a good sign. ARTICLES OF DRESS, white, innocence; black, death of a friend; dirty or torn, misfortune. APPLES, long life and success. APRICOTS, health and prosperity. ATTORNEYS, hindrance of business. ASSASSIN, be on your guard. AUCTION, a bad omen. ANTS, idleness, negligence. ASPARAGUS, profit, success. ARTICHOKES, pain, embarrassment. ACORN, evil reports. AGED MAN, prudence. AGED WOMAN, scandal.

BEAR, danger; to kill one, honor and power. BLEEDING, to bleed, loss of goods and character; to draw blood of another, success in love and trade. BLIND, to be blind, losses in business, unfaithful servants. BOAT, to be alone in a boat, a bad sign; in company, success; upset in one, a most fatal omen. BRIDGE, to cross one, prosperity and success in love; a broken bridge, sudden death. BREAD, success in life. BROTHER, to see one, a speedy marriage in the family. BUILDINGS, change of residence. BULLS, defamation of character. BURNING, sudden danger. BUTCHER, misery. BANQUET, want. BAT, a bad omen. BARN, well stored, much good; empty, the reverse; burning, gain. BATHING, in clear water, happiness; in dirty water, shame and sorrow. BELLS, ringing, a speedy marriage, good news. BEES, to be stung by them, loss of character; for the rich, unlucky, but to the poor, comport. BEARD, to a man, a long full beard, good fortune; to a married woman, loss and distress; to a maid, speedy marriage. BATTLE, secret enemies. BEANS, trouble and dissention. BEETS, freedom from trouble. BURIAL, news of the living. BIRDS, singing, a journey; to catch them, profit and pleasure; a bird's nest, increase of fortune. BLOSSOMING TREES, joy and comfort. BREWING AND BAKING, an ill housewife. BROTH, to eat, profit and gain. BURIED ALIVE, to be, great wealth. BURNED, to be, riches and honor. BASKET, to men, ill; to woman, good. BONNET, to women, a new lover. BUTTONS, sadness and misfortune. BARLEY, good fortune. BALL, perfidy. BARBER, deceit. BAKER, gain. BEGGAR, unexpected help. BOTTLES, a feast; empty, sickness. BRANDY, degrading pleasure. BROOK, clear, lasting friendship; troubled, domestic quarrels. BISHOP, death of a distant relative. BURIAL, marriage. BUTTER, great surprise.

CARDS, success in love and business. CATS, trouble. CATTLE, fat, plenty; lean, scarcity. COACH, to ride in one, poverty and disgrace. COALS, burning, a good sign; extinguished, death. COOK, wedding. CORN, success. CROWN, dignity. CRUTCHES, a bad omen. CURRANTS, happiness and success in life. CHURCH, disappointment. CAKES, happiness. CHEESE, profit in trade. CHICKENS, bad luck. CLOUDS, white, a prosperous voyage; dark, anger. CATERPILLARS, danger from secret enemies. CHAINS and all kinds of jewelry are good dreams to women. CHEEKS, fat and rosy, good to all; lean and pale, grief. CART, to draw one, servi tude; to be drawn in one, others will serve you. COAL PIT, marriage with a widow. COMBING, you will better your condition. COMFORT, to the rich, injury; to the poor, aid. CROCODILE, pirates and robbers. CROSS, sadness. CHILDREN, prosperity. CLIMBING, success in life. CHERRIES, disappointment and vexation. CUCUMBERS, health to the sick, and moderate success in trade. COFFIN, death of a friend or relation. CAMEL, riches. Cow, abundance. CALF, certain gain. COCK, pride, power. CROW, a refusal. CANARY, death of a friend. CRABS, a lawsuit. CHESTNUTS, home troubles. CYPRESS, dispair. CABBAGE, health, long life. CAULIFLOWER, sickness. CAVERN, quarrel, loss. CARDINAL, unexpected gain. CARPENTER, arrangement of affairs. COBBLER, ill paid labor. CELLAR, full, renown; empty, health. CIDER, distant heritage. CHOCOLATE, illness. COFFEE, dissipation.

DISEASE, speedy employment. DRAGON, great treasures. DANCING, joyful news, success in love. DEER, war and famine. DICE, fortunate in love and trade. DIRT, sickness and dishonor. DITCHES, precipices or rocks foretell many dangers. DOGS, friendly, a lucky sign; barking and snarling, danger from secret enemies. DROWNING, good to the dreamer. DEATH, to be dead, success and speedy marriage; to see another dead, unkind usage. DRUNKENNESS, a happy marriage with wealth. DAIRY, to a maid, a rich and honored husband; to the farmer, abundant crops. DEVIL, dangers to be overcome. DRINK, cold water, good; hot, sickness; wine, good; oil, poison. DUNGHILL, success in all undertakings. DAISIES, in spring and summer, good; but bad in fall and winter. DANDELIONS, injuries from secret enemies. DUCK, profit and pleasure; to kill one, mistortune. DOVE, happiness at home. DIAMONDS, brief happiness. DOCTOR, honor, happiness. DWARF, great danger. DYER, embarrassed affairs. DINNER-PARTY, reconciliation.

EAGLE, riches and honor. EGGS, success in love and trade; broken, quarrels and poverty. ELEPHANT, riches and speedy marriage. ECLIPSE, of the moon, loss of a dear female friend; of the sun, loss of a dear male friend. EARTHQUAKE, a change of affairs. EXECUTION, you will be asked to relieve great distress.

EARS, fair and well shaped, great renown; deformed, the contrary. EATING, losses in trade and disappointment in love. ENEMY, a caution to beware. EELS, if you hold them, honor and happiness; if they escape you, disappointments. EMBROIDERY, love. EPITAPH, indiscretion.

FACE, swelled, wealth. FALL, to fall from a high place, loss of place and goods. FEET, to wash them, molestation and trouble. FAN, change of affairs. FURNITURE, to be pleased with it, health and prosperity; to display it, trouble or a funeral. FISHPOND, you will thrive. FLESH, to increase, gain; to lose it, losses. FLIES, many enemies; to kill them, a good omen. FOREST, trouble. FIELDS, health and happiness. FIGS, prosperity. FIGHTING, loss of character and property. FIRE, bright, good news; smoky, brief joy. FISH, to catch them, success in love and business; to catch none, disappointment. FINGERS, bleeding from a cut, prosperity; to lose one, loss of friends and goods. FLEAS, a bad sign; to kill them, triumph. FLOODS, great opposition from rich neighbors. FLOWERS, fresh, happiness and success; wilted, loss in trade and death in the family. FLYING, elevation of fortune, prosperous journey. FOUNTAIN, clear water, riches and honor; muddy, vexation and trouble. FOX, many difficulties. FROGS, success in love and trade. FRUITS, ripe, happiness and riches; green or out of season, sickness; rotten, poverty. FUNERAL, a speedy marriage or acquisition of wealth. FILES, profitable business. FERRY, indecision. FAIR, pickpockets and thieves. FAWN, peril. FALCON, increase of fortune. FUNERAL SERVICE, a legacy. FEATHERS, white, joy, friendship; black, loss. FRIEND, quarrel and reconciliation. FOOTMAN, dangerous journey.

GLOVES, brief pleasure. GHOST, marriage in the family; if it speaks, prepare for death. GALLOWS, riches and honor. GARDEN, elevation to fortune and dignity. GEESE, success, riches and fidelity. GIANTS, a good omen. GIFTS, to receive, some good will happen to you; to bestow, adversity. GLASS, inconstancy, bad success; broken, misfortunes. GLOBE, will become a great traveler. GOLD, success after difficulties. GOOD, to do good, pleasure;

to receive, profit and gain. GOOSEBERRIES, many children and success in your present pursuits. GRAPES, happiness and success in trade. GRAVE, to see one, sickness; to go into one, loss of property; to come out of one, a rise in the world; to help another out of one, you will save the life of a friend. GOAT, white, prosperity; black, sickness. GARLAND, hope. GRAIN, profit and gain. GAMES, at ball or top, trouble and pain. GIN, short life and many changes. GUNS, danger and adversity.

HAY, honor and influence. HILLS, assistance in difficulties. HAIL, great sorrow. HAIR, cowardice. HANDS, to work with the right, good fortune; with the left, bad luck. HANGED, a rise above your present condition. HAT, torn or dirty, damage and dishonor; one that pleases you, joy and profit. HORNS, dominion, grandeur. HORSE, running, prosperity; to see one dead, losses in business. HUNGER, to be hungry, you will gain an estate. HATRED, to hate or be hated, is ill. HEAVEN, grandeur and glory. HEAD, to have one larger than ordinary, dignity, esteem. HENS, joy and profit. HORNETS, false tongues. HOUSE, to build, a good omen; on fire, hasty news. HUNTING, trouble through false friends.

ICE, betrayed confidence. INFANT, to a woman, trouble; to a man, good. INN, poverty and want of success. INQUEST, prosperity. IDIOT, long life, pleasure and profit. IRON, damage and losses. IGNOMING, a sudden rise in the world. ILLUMINATION, war, quarrels among relatives. INJURY, many friends. INK, black, disgrace; red, good news.

JOLLITY, a good and prosperous dream. JESSAMINE, good luck. JEOPARDY, to be in, you will be fortunate. JUBILEE, a fortune left by a relation. JOCKEY, a good turn of affairs. JUG, a journey. JUNIPERBERRIES, honors and dignity. JAIL, to see others in, loss of liberty; to be in jail, a higher station in life. JEWELS, on the road to happiness. JURY, romantic adventures. JUDGE, punishment. JEW, trickery.

KILL, to kill someone, success in business; to be killed, loss to him who killed you. KEYS, favorable to those in trade; to find one, an addition to your estate; to lose one, vexation. KNIVES, poverty, disgrace. KISSING, to kiss the living, great store of good cheer; to kiss the dead, long life. KITE, danger from thieves. KITCHEN, arrival of a friend.

LADDER, to ascend one, honor; to descend, damage. LAMB, to see one, comfort; to feed or kill one, torment. LEAPING, many difficulties. LEGS, scabby or itchy, trouble and care; a wooden leg, from good to bad. LETTERS, to receive, true love; to write, success. LEOPARDS, ostentation; to surprise one, pride brought down; to pursue one, triumph over evil reports. LETTUCE, difficulties. LEMONS, quarrels in the family. LION, future dignity; to kill one, rapid fortune; to hear one roar, danger. LOOKING-GLASS, children to the married; to the unmarried, a lover. LEAP-YEAR, the best and most lucky of dreams. LANDS, joy, riches, and a happy marriage. LANTERN, sickness and poverty. LAUREL, victory and pleasure. LAW, expense and trouble. LIZARD, ill luck through secret enemies. LOGS, the call of a stranger. LIGHT, honor and riches. LIGHTNING, change of place. LILIES, in season, a good sign; out of season, blasted hopes. LINEN, clean, glad tidings; dirty, poverty and disappointment. LEAN, to be, lawsuits, sickness. LICE, to kill them, great riches and deliverance from enemies. LYING, to lie is a bad omen. LAKE, peaceful, content; rough, trouble. LEGACY, to receive one, debts and unhappiness. LAUGHING, sorrow and weeping. LAMP, burning, prosperity; extinguished, death of a friend. LOSSES, a gift, pleasant news. LIQUORS, speedy good fortune. LAWYER, a friend's marriage. LOCKSMITH, robbery. LAME MAN, misfortune.

MALICE, pleasant prospects. MANSION, expect some calamity. MARKET, good to those in trade. MARRIAGE, death, poverty, misfortune. MILK, profit; to spill it, unlucky. MADNESS, long life, riches. MICE, success in love and prosperity. MEAT, loss and damage. MEASLES, profit and wealth through infamy. MIRE, toil and trouble to be overcome. MONKEYS, deceit, malice. MOUNTAINS, to ascend, you will become rich and arrive at great honors. MUSIC, pleasant, joyful news; unpleasant, trouble and vexation. MONEY, to receive, speedy marriage; to lose, deceit. MOON, sudden joy; overclouded, sickness. MOTHER, to see her living, joy; dead, misfortune. MELONS, to the sick, recovery. MONUMENTS, to the sick, speedy recovery; to the healthy, good luck. MAD DOG, success will crown your efforts. MURDER, tidings from a long absent friend. MUSICIAN, peace and comfort. MULE, obstinacy. MILLS, a legacy from a relation. MIRROR, treason; broken, death of a child. MUSTARD, quarrels. MONEY LENDER, persecution.

NAKEDNESS, to see a man naked, fear; a fair, handsome woman, honor and joy; an ill made woman, shame, ill luck. NIGHT WALKS, trouble and melancholy. NUTMEGS, many changes. NAVIGATION, ship or boat, danger. NEGROES, ominous of evil. NOSE, to have a large one, prosperous affairs. NOSEGAY, withered hopes. NAILS, long growing nails, riches and happiness. NUTS, to see them, wealth; to crack them, unfaithfulness. NEEDLES, to a woman, a pleasant journey; to a man, perplexity.

OLIVES, dignities, success. ONIONS, domestic strife. OYSTERS, gluttony, low pleasures. OCEAN, to one about to go on a journey, a lucky sign. ORPHANS, profits and riches from a stranger. OFFICE, to be turned out of, death and loss of property. OIL, to be annointed with, to a woman, good fortune; to a man, shame. OVEN, a hot oven, change of place. OWL, sickness and poverty. ORANGES, wounds, grief. ORGAN, joy. ORCHARD, riches, affection and constancy. OFFEND, if others offend you, a long journey to a friend; to offend, a visit from a friend. OPERA, pleasure followed by pain.

PAIN, to suffer, glad tidings from the absent. PASSION, to be in a passion, sickness, perhaps death; to have others in a passion with you, good fortune. PEDESTRIAN, to journey on foot, hardships, false friends, loss of money. PEDDLER, hypocritical friends. PHYSICIAN, true love. PLEASURE, to enjoy, difficulties. PUZZLE, to be puzzled, expect a great favor from some one. PLOUGHING, a good sign. PEACHES, health, contentment. PEARS, success in business. PIES, joy and profit. PIGEON, to see them, is good.

PINE TREE, idleness. PILE, to pile up, assistance in business. PRAYER, to pray, happiness. PIT, to fall in, heavy misfortunes; to climb out of one, will overcome difficulties and become rich. PURSE, to find one, unlooked for prosperity; to lose one, loss of a friend. PLUMS, loss of goods and reputation. POND, joy and success. PRECIPICE, injury to person and goods. PRISONERS, courage. PATHS, straight, happiness in work; crooked, much ill. PHEASANT, good fortune; to kill one, peril. PEACOCK, pride, vanity; screaming, a storm. PICTURES, domestic felicity. PORCUPINE, business troubles. PIGS, assured gain. PEAS, good luck. PALM, honor, power, vic'ory. PEARLS, tears. PINS, contradiction. POSTMAN, tidings of a friend. PAPER, tidings from relatives; colored, deceit; painted, short happiness. PENS, a letter to come.

QUAILS, bad news. QUICKSILVER, trouble and discontent in the family. QUINCES, a change for the better. QUILTING, a good and lucky omen. QUARRELING, unexpected news; between lovers, lasting affection. QUEEN, prosperity.

RADISHES, discovery of secrets. RAIN, favorable to lovers. RATS, many enemies. RIDING, with a woman, very fortunate. RING, on the finger good; to fall off, evil. READING, success in love and trade. RICE, instruction. RACING, to run a race, success in life; to ride one, disappointment and anger. RAINBOW, change, great traveling, agreeable news. RASPBERRIES, a happy marriage and good news from beyond the sea. RAVENS, mischief. RIVER, success and riches. RHINOCEROS, success in business, but disappointment in love. RHUBARB, you will make friends of your enemies. RABBITS, to see them, a speedy marriage; to shoot them, sorrow and distress; white, friendship. RAGGED, to be, a higher position in society. ROWING, success in love and business. RUN, a good sign. REPTILE, cunning and dangerous enemies. ROSES, always a happy omen; full blown, health, joy; white, innocence; red, satisfaction, yellow, jealousy. REAPER, a picnic party. ROCKS, annoyances; to climb over, difficulties overcome. RIBBONS, prodigality. RIVAL, family quarrels. ROAST MEAT, a kind reception.

SCORPIONS, ill luck. SAVIOR, vindication and honor. SCANDAL, an unexpected legacy. SCARED, pleasing intelligence, separation, unexpected enjoyment. SICKNESS, to be sick, idleness, want of work; to comfort the sick, profit and felicity. SPARROWS, good ortune. SPIRIT, in white, consolation; deformed and black, deceit and temptation. SERPENT, to see them, danger, sickness, hatred; to kill one, you will overcome your enemies. STRANGE PLACE, a legacy. STARCHING, success, pleasant news. SQUIRREL, slander by enemies, quarrels. SLEEP, evil to all. SOLD, good to the poor; to the rich, ill. SOLDIERS, persecution and law suits. SPINNING, diligence and industry. SON, damage. STATUES, riches. STINGS, grief and care. SHIPWRECK, danger to all. SISTER, long life. SHAVING, loss of goods and business. SHEEP, success. SURPRISE, good luck. SYCAMORE, jealousy. STRAWBERRIES, to a maid, speedy marriage; to a youth, a sweet tempered wife; to the tradesman and farmer, wealth. SUN, to see it rise, riches and honor; to see it set, infidelity, loss of business; under a cloud, trouble and hardships. SWALLOWS, success in trade and love. SWIMMING, with your head above water, great success; under water, trouble and bad news. SHOOTING, to kill much game, success and riches; little or no game, bad luck; with bow and arrow, a good sign to the tradesman. SILK, prosperity. SCABS, to be covered with them, success and riches. SEA, a good dream to travelers. SHIP, prosperity. SHOES, to lose one, pain, sickness. SILVER, loss, deceit. SPECTRE, certain good luck. SINGING, to sing, weeping; to hear others sing, consolation and recovery. SMALL POX, profit and wealth. SNOW, a good omen. STARS, clear and bright, good news and prosperity; dusky and pale, mischief; to see them vanish, poverty and death. SPLENDOR, affliction and perhaps death. STEALING, to be accused of, a present. STORM, reconciliation. STOCKINGS, to darn, glad news; to. lose, trouble and distress. SUCCESS, death of a friend. SWAN, joy and health; to hear one sing, death. SWINE, lazy and covetous people; to trade in, sickness. SWORDS, misfortune. SERENADE, news of a marriage. STRANGE BED, security. STRANGE ROOM, success. SUPPER, news of a birth. SALT, wisdom. SUGAR PLUMS, reverses. SARDINES, treachery. SALAD, embarrassment. SOUP, return of health and fortune. SAUSAGE, affliction. SCULPTOR, profit. SAILOR, tidings from over the sea. SHEPHERD, malice. SCISSORS, enemies. SERMON, weariness. SKY, pure, a peaceful life; clouded, misfortune. STRAW, poverty. SALMON, deceit. SNAILS, infidelity. SPIDER, at night, success, money; in the morning, a law suit; to kill one, pleasure. STORKS, robbery; in winter, a great misfortune. SHEEP, great gain. STAG, gain; to kill one, scandal; to chase one, loss.

TALKING, to talk loud, trouble; to hear others talk, a good proposal. TEARS, happiness. THORNS, triumph over enemies. THROAT, injury. TORCH, burning, honor and joy; extinguished, sickness and proverty. TELESCOPE, news from a distant friend. THIRST, to quench with clear water, joy and wealth; troubled or dirty, affliction. TEETH, to lose, trouble and death of a friend; to cut new teeth, birth of a child who will become famous. THUNDER, to the rich, affliction; to the poor, repose. TRAVELING, through woods and bushes, many troubles; over hills and mountains, advancement with many difficulties. TREES, to fell, loss; to climb, future honor; withered trees, deceit; trees bearing fruit, gain. TEMPEST, after many difficulties, much happiness. THUNDER AND LIGHTNING, success in trade and love. TOADS, enemies and loss of goods. TOMBS, speedy marriage, success, unexpected news. TRUMPET to hear one, trouble and misfortune. TARTS, joy and delight. TREASURE, to find one, betrayal and losses. TURNIPS, riches and honor in the state. TURKEYS, overcoming of enemies. TEA POT, new frendship. TURTLE, delay. TAILOR, infidelity. TEA, rest. TUMBLER, to break one, a revealing of secrets; to drink from a clean one, health; a dirty one, illness.

UGLY, to be, pleasing news from an absent friend. UNDERTAKER, a speedy marriage.

VERMIN, gain of property through the death of a relative. VILLAINY, a fortune left to you by a stranger. VELVET, profit and joy. VOTE, a bad sign to the sick. VULTURE, recovery to the sick. VICTUALS, loss. VINES, health and wealth. VINEGAR, sickness. VIOLIN, good news and domestic happiness. VOMIT, to the poor, profit; to the rich, hurt. VENISON, change of affairs, VOLCANO, peace and happiness. VEAL, success. VEGETABLES, toil, quarrels. THE VINTAGE, great gain. VIOLET, success. WALKING, sickness, grief. WAR, trouble, danger. WASHING, riches, prosperity. WEDDING, sudden death. WANT, good fortune. WATER MILL, increase of business. WASP, envy, trouble. WHALES, greatness, long life. WILD BOAR, furious enemy. WHEAT, riches, prosperity. WOOD, happiness, riches, respectability. WOOL, success in trade. WILL, to make your will, long life and happiness. WALNUTS, difficulties. WELL, marriage with wealth; to fall into, peril. WOUNDS, success, profit. WAGES, to have them reduced, advancement; to have them raised, loss of position. WAVES, difficulties, distress. WALTZING, unpleasant treatment. WIDOW, comfort, happiness, WORMS, death of some dear one. WRATH, death to the dreamer or some dear one. WEASEL, cunning. WRECK, deceit. WOLF, enmity; to kill one, success; to pursue one, danger averted. WHIRL WIND, danger, scandal. WATCH, good employment. WOMAN, deceit; fair, love; ugly, scandal. WINE, prosperity; to spill, disaster.

YEAST, large family of children.

ZODIAC, to a man, travels in distant lands; to a woman, marriage with a foreigner skilled in astronomy. ZEBRA, betrayal by a friend.

FORTUNE TELLING TABLETS

AS USED BY THE EGYPTIAN MAGI OR ASTROLOGERS. A METHOD OF
TELLING FORTUNES SUPERIOR TO ALL OTHERS.

RULE.—The person whose fortune is to be told is to prick with
a pin or other sharp point on any letter they choose in the first
tablet, but by chance with the eyes shut or averted; then refer to
the second tablet to the letter under which is the magical figure
and has reference to the oracle in the following pages, which will
determine the fortune of the inquirer.

TABLET No. 1.

			A		C		D			
		Z	F	X	L	N	A			
	P	N	O	C	D	L	Q			
	Y	R	S	T	E	H	G	L		
	K	V	W	T	S	V	A	N	M	
C	D	P	O	R	B	W	X	A	C	H
B	I	Ẋ	F	G	S	B.	H	L	K	
	W	V	U	O	F	T	S	V	D	
	L	M	X	Z	A	B	W			
	B	B	L	M	O	N				
		Q	S	Y						

Tablet No. 2.

		A	B	C		
		25	15	5		
D	E	F	G	H	I	
14	16	6	13	7	18	
K	L	M	N	O	P	Q
8	17	1	9	10	22	3
R	S	T	U	V	W	
12	28	19	24	2	4	
	X	Y	Z			
	20	21	11			

ORACLE TO THE TABLETS.

GOOD FORTUNE.

1. This number, to a man, assures him, if single, a homely wife, but rich; if married, an access of riches, numerous children, and good old age. To a lady, a faithful lover and speedy marriage.

3. Very good fortune, sudden prosperity, great respect from high personages, and a letter bringing important news.

7. To a woman, if single, a good and wealthy husband; if married, a faithful partner. To a man, the same.

8. A general good sign, and your present expectations will be fulfilled.

9. To the married, if under fifty, let them not despair of a young family; to the single, sudden marriage.

10. A friend has crossed the sea and will bring home some riches, by which the party will be much benefited.

12. You will be successful in all your undertakings.

15. You may be poor and thought insignificant, but let your friends assist you and they will reap much benefit thereby.

16. A sudden journey with a pleasant fellow traveler, the result of which will be very beneficial.

18. A sudden acquaintance with the opposite sex, which will be opposed; but persevere, it will be to your advantage.

21. An important letter announcing the death of a relation, who has left you a legacy.

22. Be prudent in your conduct; much depends on yourself; it is generally a good number.

BAD FORTUNE.

2. Loss of a friend, bad success at law, loss of money, unfaithful lovers, and a bad partner.

4. A letter announcing the loss of money.

5. You will soon lose something good by passion.

6. Bad success; you will hardly succeed in any of your undertakings.

11. Suspect the fidelity of your partner, if married; if single, you are deceived.

13. You want to borrow money, but will not be able to do so.

14. The old man you have depended upon is going to be married and will have children of his own.

17. You pretend to despise these tablets, but you rely much upon them, and you may depend on it, that you will be brought to disgrace.

19. Look well to those who owe you money, if ever so little; expect a letter of abuse.

20. A drunken partner, and bad success in trade; you will never be very poor, but never very happy.

25. Look well to your conduct; justice, though slow, it is sure to overtake the wicked.

FORTUNE TELLING

Pour the grounds of tea or coffee into a white cup; shake them well about, so as to spread them over the surface; reverse the cup to drain away the superfluous contents, and then exercise your fancy in discovering what the figures thus formed represent.

Long wavy lines denote vexation and losses, their importance depending on the number of lines. Straight lines foretell peace and long life. Human figures are good omens, announcing love affairs and marriage. Circular figures indicate the reception of money. Squares foretell peace and happiness. Oblong figures, family discord. Curved, twisted or angular figures are certain signs of vexation and annoyance. A crown signifies honor. A cross, news of a death. A ring, marriage; if a letter can be discovered near it, that will be the initial of your future spouse. If the ring is in the clear part of the cup, it foretells a happy union; if clouds are about it, the contrary; if at the bottom, no marriage will take place A clover leaf, speedy good fortune, which will be more or less distant in case it appears at or near the bottom. The anchor, if at the bottom denotes success in business; at the top and in the clear part, love and fidelity; but in thick or cloudy parts, inconstancy.

The serpent is always the sign of an enemy, and if in the cloudy part, gives warning that great prudence will be necessary to ward off misfortune.

The coffin portends news of a death or long illness. The dog at the top of the cup denotes true friends; in the middle, that they are not to be trusted; but at the bottom, that they are secret enemies.

The lily, at the top, foretells a happy marriage; at the bottom, anger.

A letter signifies news; if in the clear, welcome news; surrounded by dots, a remittance of money; but if hemmed in by clouds, bad tidings and losses; a heart near it denotes a love letter.

A single tree portends restoration to health; a group of trees, misfortune, which may be avoided; several trees, wide apart, promise that your wishes will be accomplished; if encompassed by dashes, it is a token that your fortune is in its blossom, and only requires care to bring it to maturity; if surrounded by dots, riches.

Mountains signify either friends or enemies, according to their situation.

The sun, moon and stars, denote happiness and success.

The clouds, happiness or misfortune, according as they are bright or dark.

Birds are good omens, but quadrupeds, with the exception of the dog, foretell trouble and difficulties.

Fish imply good news from across the water.

A triangle portends an unexpected legacy.

A single straight line, a journey.

The figure of a man indicates a visitor; if the arm is outstretched, a present; when the figure is very distinct it shows that the visitor will be dark complexioned, and vice versa.

A crown near a cross indicates a large fortune, resulting from a death.

Flowers are signs of joy, happiness and a peaceful life.

A heart surrounded by dots, signifies joy occasioned by the receipt of money; with a ring near it, approaching marriage.

HOW TO READ YOUR FORTUNE BY THE WHITE OF AN EGG.

Break a new laid egg, and carefully separating the yolk from the white, drop the latter into a large tumbler half full of water; place this uncovered, in some dry place, and let it remain untouched for twenty-four hours, by which time the white of the egg will have formed itself into various figures, rounds, squares, ovals, animals, trees, crosses, etc., which are to be interpreted in the same manner as those formed by the coffee grounds. Of course the more whites there are in the glass, the more figures there will be.

SYNOPSIS OF HISTORICAL EVENTS DURING THE LAST HUNDRED YEARS.

1789. . Washington made first President of the U. S., John Adams, Vice-President, April 30. Thomas Jefferson, Secretary of State. First French Revolution, National Assembly constituted at Versailles May 5. Storming of the Bastille July 14. Insurrection of the Netherlands in September. Austrians driven from the Netherlands in December.

1790. Rhode Island ratifies the Constitution. Seat of the National Government at Philadelphia. End of the Belgium Republic December 10. United States Bank established December 13. City of Washington founded.

1791. John Wesley dies March 2. Louis XVI flies from Paris, arrested at Varennes, brought back June 21. Louis accepts the Constitution completed by the National Assembly, September 14. Vermont admitted into the Union.

1792. Gustavus III, of Sweden, assassinated March 16, succeeded by Gustavus IV. Procession of the "Black Breeches" invades the National Assembly and Tuileries June 20. Tuileries attacked, and Swiss guards massacred August 10. Louis and family imprisoned in the temple August 13. France invaded August 18. September massacres at Paris September 2-3. Royalty abolished September 21. Republic proclaimed September 22. John Adams re-elected Vice-President U. S. Kentucky admitted into the Union.

1793. Louis XVI executed January 21. Washington re-elected President U. S. March 4. Reign of terror in Paris. Charlotte Corday assassinates Marat July 13. Execution of Charlotte Corday July 17. Marie Antoinette, Queen of France, executed October 15. Worship of Reason introduced November 10.

1794. Koscinsko active in Poland. Danton and others executed in Paris April 6. Lord Howe defeats the French fleet off Brest June 1. Fall of Robespierre and end of the reign of terror in

Paris July 27. Russians enter Warsaw November 9. English driven out of Holland in December.

1795. Partition of Poland between Russia, Austria and Prussia January 3. Peace of Basel between Prussia and the French Republic. Insurrection at Paris May 20-21.

1796. Battle of Lodi May 10. Napoleon enters Milan May 15; Bologna June 18. Washington resigns September 17. Tennessee admitted into the Union.

1797. Battle of Rivoli January 14. Mantua capitulates to Napoleon February 1-2. John Adams, second President U. S., March 4. Napoleon takes Venice May 16.

1798. French occupy Rome February 10. It is proclaimed a Republic February 15. French take Malta June 11; invade Egypt July 1. Battle of the Pyramids July 21. Battle of the Nile August 1-2. King of Sardinia abdicates December 9.

1799. French take Ehrenbreitstein January 29. Invade Syria February. Besiege Acre March 16-May 21. Massacre of Jaffa March 27. Ferdinand the IV, of Naples, restored July 27. French enter Zurich September 26. Lose Rome September 30. Napoleon elected first Consul December 24. Washington dies December 14.

1800. Napoleon's Passage of the Great St. Bernard, May 17 -20. Battle of Marengo June 14. English take Malta September 5. Battle of Hohenlinden, December 3.

1801. Thomas Jefferson elected President U. S. March 4, Aaron Burr Vice-President. Paul, Emperor of Russia, murdered March 24. Alexander I succeeds. Nelson defeats the Danish Fleet at Copenhagen April 2. French evacuate Egypt September 2. First Census of Great Britain taken.

1802. French take St. Domingo May 7. Peace of Amiens March 27. Napoleon declared first Consul for life August 3. Ohio admitted into the Union.

1803. English evacuate Egypt March 17. Napoleon sells Louisiana to the U. S. April 30. England declares war against France May 18. French take Hannover in June. Robert Emmet heads the Irish rebellion July 23. St. Domingo proclaimed independent November 29.

1804. Napoleon becomes Emperor of France May 18. George Clinton, Vice-President U. S. Wm. Pitt appointed Prime Minister the second time May 12. Alexander Hamilton killed in a duel July 12. The Pope crowns Napoleon and Josephine December 2.

1805. Thomas Jefferson, President U. S., March 4 (second term). Third co-alition against France completed September 8. French defeat the Austrians at Ulin October 17-19. English defeat French at Trafalgar October 21. French occupy Vienna November 13. Battle of Austerlitz December 2. Peace of Presburg December 26.

1806. Conspiracy of Aaron Burr. English destroy the French Squadron of St. Domingo February 6. Fourth co-alition against France October 6. Battles of Jena and Anerstadt October 14. Napoleon enters Berlin October 27. French occupy Hamberg in November..

1807. Battle of Eylan February 7-8. Slave trade in the British Empire abolished March 25. Peace of Tilsit July 7. Cardinal York, the last of the Stuarts, dies July 13. French enter Lisbon November 30. Napoleon enters Spain, seizes Etruria December 10. First Steamboat on the Hudson.

1808. Clinton re-elected Vice-President U. S. Napoleon occupies Rome February 2. Creates a new nobility in France March 11. Murat enters Madrid March 23. Joseph Bonaparte made King of Spain June 6. Murat made King of Naples July 15. Spanish inquisition abolished December 4. Finland incorporated with Russia.

1809. Battle of Corunna. Austrians invade Bavaria August 11. Napoleon enters Vienna May 13. Battle of Wagram July 6. Empress Josephine divorced December 15.

1810. Napoleon marries Marie Louisa, of Austria, April 1. English take Mauritius December 3. University of Berlin founded.

1811.   Mamdukes massacred at Cairo March 10.   Battle of Tippecanoe November 11.   Great Comet visible for four months.

1812.   Louisiana admitted into the Union in April.   U. S. declare war against Great Britain June 18.   Napoleon declares war against Russia June 22.   Enters and burns Moskow September 11.   Evacutes Moskow October 19.

1813.   Fifth co-alition against France March 1.   James Madison President U. S. (second term).   Battle of Lutzen May 2.   Of Bantzen May 20-21.   Battle of Vittoria June 21.   Battle of the Pyrenees July 25-30.   Battle of Dresden August 24-27.   Wellington invades France October 7.   Battle of Leipsic October 16-19.   French evacuate Germany November 22.

1814.   Paris capitulates March 31.   Senate deposes Napoleon April 1.   Battle of Toulouse April 10.   Napoleon abdicates April 11.   Lands in Elba May 4.   Peace of Paris May 30.   U. S. invade Canada in July.   Capture and burning of Washington by Gen. Ross August 24.   Peace of Ghent between England and the U. S. December 24.   English attack New Orleans December 27.

1815.   Battle of New Orleans, English defeated January 8. Napolean escapes from Elba February 26; enters Paris March 20. Battles of Ligny and Quatre Bras June 16.   Battle of Waterloo June 18.   Allies enter Paris July 7.   Napoleon surrenders to H. M. S. Bellerophon July 15; arrives at St. Helena October 16.   Second peace of Paris November 20.   Chamber of Peers condemns Marshal Ney December 6; he is shot at Paris December 7.

1816.   Admiral Lord Hood dies June 27.   Indiana admitted into tne Union December 11.   Ronalds invents the electric telegraph.

1817.   James Monroe, President U. S. March 4.   Pius the VII condemns the Bible by Bull of June 29.   Koscinsco dies October 15.   Mississippi admitted into the Union in December.

1818.   Queen Charlotte of England dies November 17.   Illinois admitted into the Union December 3.

1819.   Spain secedes Florida to the U. S. February 22.   Princess Victoria born May 24. Macadams' system of road-making published. Alabama admitted into the Union December 14.

1820. George IV declared King of England January 29. Maine admitted into the Union March 15. Jesuits expelled from Russia March 25.

1821. Missouri compromise passed February 28. James Monroe, President U. S., March 4, (second term). Insurrection in Greece March 6. Greek Patriarch hung at Constantinople April 21. Independence of Brazil proclaimed April 22. Napoleon dies at St. Helena May 5. Missouri admitted into the Union August 10. Rise of the Slavery Agitation in the U. S.

1822. Greeks declare their Independence January 1. Massacre of Scio April–May. Greeks take Athens June 22. Don Pedro declared Emperor of Brazil October 12.

1823. French invade Spain April 7; enter Madrid May 23. British Anti-Slavery Society founded. Joseph Smith originates Mormonism.

1824. War with Burmah, Lord Byron dies April 18. Lafayette visits U. S. August 15.

1825. John Quincy Adams, President U. S., March 4. Great earthquake in Algiers March 2–7. Commercial panic in England in December. First voyage by steam from England to India.

1826. Don Pedro, Emperor of Brazil, becomes King of Portugal March 10. Adams and Jefferson Ex-Presidents of the U. S., died July 4.

1827. Frederick, Duke of York, dies January 5. Charles X, of France, disbands the National Guards April 29. Battle of Navarino October 26. Dreyse invents the needle gun. Omnibus introduced into Paris.

1828. Peace between Brazil and Buenos Ayres August 29. Lord Liverpool dies December 4. New corn law in England. Peels sliding scale established.

1829. Great political excitement in the U. S. Andrew Jackson, President, March 4. Greeks take Lepanto May 9. Peace of Adrianople September 14.

1830. Allied powers declare the independence of Greece February 3. The Porte acknowledges it April 25. William IV declared King of England June 26. Charles X flies from Paris July 30; abdicates August 2. Louis proclaimed King of France August 9.

1831. Revolution in Brazil. Emperor Pedro abdicates April 7. William IV and Queen Adelaide crowned September 9. Asiatic cholera in England in November–December.

1832. Goethe dies March 22. Prince Otto, of Bavaria, proclaimed King of Greece August 3. Sir Walter Scott dies September 21. Heathcote's steam plough patented.

1833. Andrew Jackson, President U. S. (second term) March 4. Santa Anna, President of the Mexican Republic, April 18. Slavery abolished in the British Colonies August 28.

1834. Lafayette dies May 30. Houses of Parliament burned October 16.

1835. Texas revolts against Mexico. Independence of Texas proclaimed December 22. Colts' revolver patented. Halley's Comet appears. The Seminole war in Florida.

1836. Arkansas admitted into the Union. Charles X, of France, dies November 6.

1837. Martin Van Buren, President U. S. March 4. Victoria declared Queen of England June 20. Cholera rages on the continent July–August. Winter Palace, St. Petersburg, burned December 29. Father Mathews' temperance mission begins. Financial crisis in the U. S.

1838. Royal Exchange, London, burned January 10. Queen Victoria crowned June 28. End of the rebellion in Canada in November. Daguerreotype process discovered.

1839. The Pope prohibits the slave trade December 3. First English settlement in New Zealand. Gold discovered in Australia.

1840. Queen Victoria marries Prince Albert February 10. Remains of Napoleon landed at Cherbourg November 30. Deposited in the Hotel des Invalides December 15.

1841. Union of Upper and Lower Canada proclaimed February 10. Gen. Harrison, President U. S., March 4. He dies April 4. Vice-President John Tyler succeeds him. The President vetoes the U. S. bank bill, and the entire cabinet resigns September 11. Mormon Temple at Nanvoo founded. London Punch begun.

1842. Great Fire at Hamburg May 5-7. The Boers of Natal defeated June 26. The French take Tahiti September 8. Steam hammer patented. Illustrated London News begun.

1843. Appearance of great comet in March. Natal annexed to Cape Colony in May. Botta discovers the site of Nineveh. Opening of the great Thames Tunnel. The Dorr Rebellion in the U. S.

1844. First Telegraph line established in the U. S. May 27. Joseph Smith, the Mormon prophet, murdered June 27. Brigham Young succeeds him.

1845. Iowa and Florida admitted into the Union March 1. James K. Polk, President U. S., March 4. Sir John Franklin's last expedition May 23. Mexico declares war against the U. S. June 4. Texas admitted into the Union December 27. Railway mania and panic in England.

1846. Famine in Ireland. Gen. Taylor defeats the Mexicans at Palo Alto May 8. At Resaca de la Palma May 9. Santa Fe annexed to the U. S. August 23. Gen. Taylor takes Monterey September 24.

1847. Mexicans defeated at Buena Vista February 22-23. Gen. Scott takes Vera Cruz March 28. Enters Jalapa April 19. Sir John Franklin dies June 11. Gen. Scott takes Mexico September 14-15. Mormons found Salt Lake City.

1848. Insurrection at Mesina January 6. Gold discovered in California in January. John Quincy Adams dies February 21. Louis Philip, of France, abdicated February 24. Income tax riots in London March 6-7. Revolution in Vienna. Prince Metternich flies March 13. Insurrection in Berlin March 17. At Milan March 18. King of Bavaria abdicates March 21. Sicilian Parliament deposes King Ferdinand April 13. Treaty of peace between Mexico and the U. S. May 19. Wisconsin admitted into the Union May 29. Insurrection at Paris, the Archbishop of Paris shot while mediating June 26. Vienna in revolt, the Emperor flies October 7. Louis Napoleon, President of the French Republic December 20.

1849. Republic proclaimed at Rome February 8. Great gold rush to California. Gen. Taylor President of the U. S. March 4. Kossuth Governor of Hungary April 4. French besiege Rome June 3. Fighting in Paris June 14. Russians invade Hungary June 17. The French take Rome July 3. Cholera in London. Livingston discovers Lake N'Gamir.

1850. President Taylor dies July 9. Fillmore succeeds him. Burning of Cracow July 18. Louis Philip dies August 26. California admitted into the Union September 9. Fugitive slave law passed September 18. First submarine telegraph between France and England.

1851. Austrians hold Hamburg January 29. Gold digging begun in Australia February. Prince Metternich returns to Vienna September 23. Coup D'Etat at Paris December 2-3. Louis Napoleon President of the French Republic for ten years December 20-21.

1852. Louis Napoleon publishes new constitution. Henry Clay dies June 29; the Duke of Wellington September 14; Daniel Webster October 21.

1853. Revolution in Mexico. Louis Napoleon marries Eugenia De Montigo January 29. Franklin Pierce President U. S. March 4. Santa Anna President of Mexico April 1. English and French fleets enter Dardanelles October 22. War between Russia and Turkey October 23.

1854. French and English fleets enter Black Sea January 4. Treaty between the U. S. and Japan March 23. France declares war against Russia March 28. Troubles in Kansas, March and April. Kansas-Nebraska bill passed in May. Allies land in the Crimea September 14. Sebastopol bombarded October 17. Bat-

tle of Balaklava October 25. Battle of Inkerman November 5.
First Armstrong gun made.

1855. Sardinia joins the Allies January 26. Emperor of Rus-
sia Nicholas dies March 2. Universal exhibition at Paris opened
May 15. Battle of the Tchernaya August 16. Malakoff and
Redan stormed September 8. Russians evacuate south side of
Sebastopol and are defeated at Kars September 29. Niagara sus-
pension bridge completed.

1856. Free State Legislature in Kansas constituted March
4. Treaty of Paris March 30. Kansas refused admission into
the Union April 11. Allies evacuate the Crimea July 12. Alexander II of Russia crowned September 7. Organization of the
republican party. Nomination of John C. Fremont.

1857. Archbishop of Paris assassinated January 3. Dred
Scott Decision in March. James Buchanan President U. S. March
4. Europeans at Cawnpore surrender to Nana Sahib June 25.
Mormon Rebellion May and June. Massacre of women and
children at Cawnpore July 15. Gen. Havelock enters Cawnpore
July 17. Attempt to lay Atlantic cable fails August 11. Relief of
Lucknow by Gen. Havelock September 25. Lucknow rescued by
Sir Colin Campbell November 22. Canton taken by the French
and English December 28-29. Civil war in Kansas in December.

1858. Attempt to assassinate Louis Napoleon January 14.
Lucknow taken March 19-20. Minnesota admitted into the
Union May 11. Great eruption of Vesuvius May 21. First At-
lantic cable completed and first message received August 20.

1859. Oregon admitted into the Union February 12. Revo-
lution at Florence April 27. Victor Emanuel declares war against
Austria April 27; France against Austria May 3. Alexander
Von Humbolt dies May 6. Battle of Montebello May 20. Bat-
tle of Magenta June 4. Napoleon and Victor Emanuel enter Milan
June 8. Battle of Solferino June 24. Negro insurrection at Har-
per's Ferry under John Brown October 17. Brown hanged
December 2.

1860. Garibaldi takes Palermo May 27. Great Eastern crosses Atlantic June 17-27. Battle of Melazzo June 20. Insurrection at Naples August 17. Garibaldi enters Naples September 8, and proclaims Victor Emanuel King of Italy. South Carolina secedes December 20. Oil wells discovered in Pennsylvania.

1861. Williams I King of Prussia January 2. Mississippi seceded January 9, followed by Florida, Alabama, Georgia, Louisiana, Texas, Virginia, Arkansas, Tennessee and North Carolina. Kansas admitted into the Union January 29. Russian Serfs emancipated March 3. Abraham Lincoln President of U. S. March 4. Confederates take Fort Sumpter April 12-13. Confederate Congress meets at Richmond July 20. First Battle of Bull Run July 21. Specie payment suspended in the federal states December 31.

1862. Encounter of Merrimac and Monitor in James River May 9. France declares war against Mexico April 16. Federals take New Orleans April 24. Battles on the Chickahominy June 25-July 1. Battle of South Mountain September 14. At Antietam September 19. Battle at Fredericksburg December 13.

1863. Emancipation proclamation January 1. West Virginia made a state January 1. Insurrection in Poland January 22. Stonewall Jackson mortally wounded at Chancellorsville May 2; dies May 9. Grant takes Vicksburg July 4. The French enter Mexico June 10. Battles of Gettysburg July 1-3. Federals take Fort Hudson. Maximilian of Austria, Emperor of Mexico July 19. Federals occupy Chattanooga September 10. First Fenian Congress meets at Chicago November 25.

1864. Garibaldi visits England in April. Maximilian arrives in Mexico May 29. The Kearsarge sinks the Alabama off Cherbourg June 19. Fugitive slave law repealed June 23. Federals hold Atlanta September 2. Nevada admitted into the Union October 31. Gen. Sherman holds Savannah December 21. Nobel introduces dynamite.

1865. Gen. Gilmore occupies Charleston February 17. President Lincoln enters on second term of office March 4. Gen. Grant takes Richmond April 3. Gen. R. E. Lee surrenders April 9. Assassination of President Lincoln April 4. Vice-president Johnson succeeds April 15. Jefferson Davis captured May 10. End of civil war. Slavery abolished in the U. S. December 10.

1866. U. S. Congress passes civil rights bill April 12. Fenian raids into Canada May 31–June 7. Prussia withdraws from the German Confederation June 14. Enters Saxony and Hanover June 15. Austria declares war June 17; Prussia June 18; Italy June 20. Hanoverian army surrenders June 29. Prussians defeat Austrians at Sadowa July 3; occupy Frankfort July 16. Treaty of Prague August 28.

1867. First ship passes through Suez Canal February 17. Fenian agitation in Ireland February–March. Nebraska admitted into the Union March 1. Alaska ceded to the U.S. French evacuate Mexico March 16. Dominion of Canada constituted March 29. Emperor Maximilian of Mexico shot at Queretaro June 19. Juarez re-elected President of Mexico in October. Annexation of Cochin China to France.

1868. President Johnson impeached February 25. James Buchanan dies June 1. Insurrection in Spain September 18. Queen Isabella leaves Spain September 30.

1869. Gen. Grant President U. S. March 4. Suez Canal formally opened November 17. Pacific Railway completed.

1870. Charles Dickens dies June 9. Isabella of Spain abdicates June 25. France declares war against Prussia July 19. Battle of Sedan September 1. Napoleon surrenders, and Freiburg capitulates September 2. Revolution at Paris, Republic proclaimed September 4. Germans invest Paris September 19. Strasburg capitulates September 28. Gen. Von der Tann takes Orleans October 11. Gen. Robert E. Lee dies October 13. Metz falls October 28. Communist Insurrection at Paris October 31. German Empire declared December 10. Tours surrenders December 21. Mont Cenis Tunnel completed.

1871. King William of Prussia proclaimed Emperor of Germany January 18. Battle of St. Quentin January 19. Paris capitulates January 28. Germans enter Paris and peace ratified March 1. Germans evacuate Paris March 3. Commune proclaimed at Paris March 28. Tuileries, Louvre etc., burned by the Communists, and Archbishop of Paris shot May 24. Insurrection ended May 28. Mont Cenis Tunnel opened September 17. Great Chicago fire October 8-10.

1872. British Columbia incorporated with the Dominion of Canada February 8. Dutch Possessions on the Gold Coast transferred to Great Britain April 6. Great eruption of Vesuvius April 24 to May 1.

1873. Louis Napoleon dies January 9. Gen. Grant President U. S. March 4 (second term.) Mac Mahon President French Republic May 24. England pays Alabama indemnity September 9. Germans evacuate French territory September 16. Marshal Bazaine tried October 6. Sentenced December 10.

1874. Coup D'Etat at Madrid January 3. Chas. Sumner dies March 11. Spain declared in a state of siege July 19. Marshal Bazaine escapes from prison August 9. Fizi Island ceded to England September 30. Alphonso, King of Spain December 30.

1875. Arctic Expedition, The "Alert" and "Discovery" Sail from Portsmouth May 29. Great floods at Toulouse June 24.

1876. Imperial Bank of Germany opened January 1. Destructive hurricanes in the west March 10. New Mexico admitted into the Union March 11. Queen Victoria proclaimed Empress of India May 1. Attempted assassination of Emperor William May 11. Sioux Indians massacre federal troops June 25. Centenary of American Independence July 4. Colorado admitted into the Union August 2.

1877. U. S. electoral commission appointed January 30. R. B. Hayes declared elected March 2, and inaugurated March 5. Great railroad strike in the U. S. July 18-30.

1878. Paris exhibiticn opened May 1. Attempted assassination of Emperor William June 2. Yellow fever rages in the Southern States September-October. Gold sells at par in Wall Street December 17.

1879. U. S. resumes specie payment January 1. Zulus defeat English in South Africa January 22. River Theiss in Hungary overflows; 60,000 persons homeless. Negro exodus from Louisiana and Mississippi to Kansas sets in April 5. Gen. Grant completes his two years tour around the world September 20.

1880. Riots in Connemara, Ireland, January 3. Winter Palace at St. Petersburg blown up by dynamite February 17. Mount St. Gothard Tunnel completed February 29. Mount Vesuvius Railway opened June 6. French Republic expels Jesuits. June 30.

1881. Chilians take Lima January 17. James A. Garfield President U. S. March 4. Alexander II of Russia assassinated March 13. Assassination of President Garfield July 2. Gen. Burnside dies September 13. Garfield dies September 19. Chester A. Arthur twenty-first President U. S. September 22. Opening of the Cotton Exhibition at Atlanta, Georgia, October 5. Centennial celebration at Yorktown October 10.

1882. Terrible railroad accident at Spuyten Duyvil, New York, January 13. Guiteau found guilty January 25; hung June 30. Transit of Venus December 6.

1883. Snow falls in San Francisco the first time in 17 years January 1. Great floods in the Western States February 3. New York and Brooklyn bridge opened May 24. Over 200,000 people cross east river bridge May 27. Telegraphers Brotherhood strike July 19-August 18. Capt. Webb the English swimmer drowned while attempting to swim the Niagara whirlpool July 24. Terrible railroad disaster at Carlyon, N. Y., July 28. Northern Pacific Railroad completed and opened for traffic September 8. Two cent letter postage goes into effect in the U. S. October 1. Great fire at Dallas, Texas, October 8. Earthquake in San Francisco October 13. Sergeant Mason pardoned November 24.

1884. Steamer City of Columbus wrecked off Gay Head, 100 lives lost, January 18. Great floods in the Ohio Valley in February. Bodies of "Jeanette" Explorers arrive in New York; imposing reception and parade February 22. Washington monument completed February 21, Grover Cleveland twenty-second President U. S. March 4. Bill passed placing Gen. Grant on retired list of the army March 4. Commencing of the great strike of the ironworkers of the west June 1. Gen. Grant dies July 23; buried at Riverside Park, New York, August 8.

1885. Great eight hour labor movement May 1. Great anarchist Haymarket riot in Chicago May 4.

1886. Terrific cyclones and storms through the west May 11-20. Earthquake in Charleston and Sumerville, S. C., both cities partially destroyed August-September 7. Ex-President C. A. Arthur dies November 18. Gen. John A. Logan dies December 26.

1887. Senate passes the Inter State Commerce act October-January 14. Signed by the president February 4. Terrible railroad accident near White River Junction, Vermont, February 5. Henry Ward Beecher dies March 8. John G. Saxe "Humorous Poet" dies March 31. The American exhibition opened in London May 9. Collision near Sandy Hook of the White Star Line Steamers Brittannic and Celtic May 19. Terrible railroad accident near Chatworth, Ills., nearly one hundred killed August 10.

1889. January 25 big street car strike in Brooklyn and New York. February 19 hotel boiler explodes in a Hartford, Ct., hotel and kills 40 of the guests. March 4 Gen. Harrison inaugurated President U. S. April 29 frightful railroad accident on the Grand Trunk Railroad near Hamilton, Ontario, 23 burned to death. May 4 Dr. P. H. Cronin murdered; his body found May 22. May 31 the great Conemaugh valley disaster or Johnstown horror; loss of life over 3,500. Burning of Seattle, W. T., January 7. Sullivan and Kilrain fight July 8. Spokane Falls, W. T., destroyed by fire August 5. August 22 Hyppotite enters Porte Au Prince, Hayti, and is declared President of the Republic. Cronin trial begins August 26. North and South Dakota admitted into the Union November 2. $10,000,000 fire in Lynn, Mass., November 26. An $8,000,000 fire in Boston November 28. November 30 Minneapolis Tribune building burned; 20 lives lost. The Russian influenza reaches the U. S. December 13. December 16 the Cronin jury bring in the ver-

dict. Great hurricane on the Samoan Islands wreck six men of war.
250 lives lost March 29. November 15 Revolution in Brazil Don
Pedro deposed and the Republic established without loss of blood.

RUNNING THE GAUNTLET.

A tall, fine looking man of thirty, with a frame whose muscular grandeur not even the ill fitting miners suit could altogether
conceal, an upright easy carriage, strong embrowned and nervous
hands, and great black eyes that lighted up a face which gave
evidence of veiled passion and sleeping strength; this is Lionel Carroll.

He was walking slowly down one of the streets of the little
mining town of Aurora, gazing with interest at the varied phases
of a life so new and strange to eastern eyes.

A white, shapely hand fell lightly on Carroll's shoulder. Wheel-
ing sharply he uttered an exclamation, and then stood still for a
moment, and stared blankly at the man before him.

Surely there was nothing striking in the appearance of the
one he had faced so abruptly—a man of medium size, with sandy
hair and beard, and strange shifting hazel eyes; but the instant
that Lionel Carroll met the glance of those changeful eyes his
mind, with the quickness of thought, reverted to the day five
years before, when Owen Bradford left the little New England village, with bitter curses on his lips against the one, who, he
declared, had robbed him of pretty Nettie Forest's love. "I hate
you Lion Carroll!—hate you!—hate you!" and the words came
hissing while hot with passion from the livid lips. "And I swear
I'll yet make you drink the very dregs of the cup of sorrow for
what you have made me suffer, so help me! The wheel turns,
and you will be at the bottom yet and then"—The sentence was
never finished, for with face hideous as a changelings, he turned
away from his successful rival.

But now Carroll could scarcely trust his eyes. There was not a trace of enmity or hard feeling in the suave smiling face, not a tinge of bitterness in the careless words, spoken with a light laugh: "Well, Carroll, you're a long time in recognizing a friend; your memory has grown treacherous, has it not not, my dear sir?"

"Not at all Bradford," answered Carroll, heartily willing to bury the past, and glad to see a familiar face. "Not at all, I was rather surprised at seeing you, for I had the impression that you were in Frisco."

"I make my headquarters there," answered Bradford carelessly, "but came over to Aurora on business. By the way, Carroll, how did you happen to be here, smitten with gold fever, eh?"

"Yes," answered Carroll, frankly, "I came out to try my luck, like thousands of others, and I got here to-day."

"Ah," and Bradford lightly stroked his blonde beard, "how did you leave all the folks in the little town where we used to vegetate? and that little daisy, Nettie Forest, about whom we had such a foolish schoolboy quarrel? But I presume she is Mrs. Carroll now; if so, you have my best wishes, etc., old boy."

How coolly it was said. Carroll was completely disarmed, and he said cordially:

"Thank you, Bradford. Nettie has been my wife for over four years, and you ought to see our boy, Bradford, he is the dearest little rogue that ever the sun shone on."

"Ah!" slowly drawled Bradford again, "so I suppose. But see here, Carroll, have you obtained anything to do yet, or made up your mind to go prospecting?"

"No," said the other, "you know I told you that I had just got here—why?" "Well I'll tell you the whole story," answered Bradford briskly. "Our company in Frisco own the Heintzelman Mine down on the Slate Range about two hundred miles from here, but for a long time we have heard nothing from it, and cannot imagine what the trouble is, so I just took a run over here with the intention of getting a few men to go over to the mine and then report to the company. Wages will be twenty dollars a day, for, I shall not deny that it may be a little risky. Perhaps you would like the chance, though, Carroll, and in case that you will, I will substantiate what I have said." Bradford drew a few papers from his breast pocket, Carroll at once preceived their truth and telling Bradford that he would think it over, soon separated from him, promising that he would see Bradford a little later.

Bradford turned and watched Carroll as he walked away with an elastic, easy stride. "Fool! Fool!" he muttered to himself, a baleful light now gleaming in the evil eyes. "How easily he was taken in? Does he judge me by himself I wonder, and therefore imagine that I soon forgive injuries? Bah! my great souled gentleman, it takes men like me to read your kind. He'll accept and I know it, but you would'nt, if you knew what I do that the mill of the Heintzelman has been destroyed and the men killed by Indians, who will serve you the same way, as surely as you go there; and then Bradford, you must go east and break the sad news to the widow."

An evil laugh broke from Bradford's lips, a low deep chuckle, too full of wickedness to ring out full and heartily, while his whole face was as colorless as rock, revealing no indications of the treachery which filled his heart.

"Boys, its my opinion that the sooner we leave this place behind us the better it will be for us, what say you?" said Lionel Carroll, quietly, turning to the trio of men standing near him.

They had ridden fast and far, those venturesome men who had taken their lives in their hands, and dared the dangers that lurked on those wild western plains; for a distance of over two hundred miles lay between them and the busy town of Aurora. And what did they find awaiting them at the end of their journey? A story of Indian treachery and death written out in black and white in the blackened timbers of the ruined mill and the whitened bones of the workmen. Dead silence brooded over the place, and yet it seemed to the little company that a voice had suddenly called to them out of this awful wilderness.

Though their stay had been but of a few moments duration they immediatly assented to Carroll's proposition.

Not an instant of rest was given horse or pack mule; but, flinging themselves into their saddles, they turned their faces toward Aurora, the Mecca of their hearts now, and the four left the ghastly place at utmost speed, as if they could not endure to breathe in its shadow.

On and on, never stopping, until the shadows of night folding down upon them, bade them draw rein by their silent yet powerful commands.

It was rather a singular place where the little party halted to spend the night; a little irregular valley, surrounded on all sides by the sentinels of centuries, which were clothed to their very rugged heads with nut pine, save at one point.

At the western and narrowest edge of the valley was a narrow gorge, torn or chiseled by mother nature through the very heart of the mountains, which led out to the main valley, or extensive desert, toward the west.

It appeared as if, at some earlier period, instead of a grass tufted valley, a little lake has nestled down in the midst of these towering mountains like a lost saphire; but at last through the broken gorge, its waters had found liberty, only to be swallowed up by the burning, thirsty sand of the western desert.

Supper was eaten without fire or light, and with the horses and mules grazing near them, the four men, lay down to rest their weary frames.

Somewhere about midnight Carroll awoke; a feeling of dread or foreboding lay heavy upon mind and soul and forbade the return of sleep.

He raised himself upon one elbow, and with his every sense strained, tried to discover if there was any foundation for the unaccountable anxiety which had fastened itself upon him.

All about him was soft, warm obscurity, unbroken by a single sound, save the low breathing of the men beside him.

A few pale stars shone faintly through the dusk; flickering as if the oil was low in the lamp, the flames was expiring in its socket.

I should be ashamed of such a cowardly feeling, he thought impatiently; it does not seem possible for noisy danger to lurk in this heavenly peace and quiet.

He was about to throw himself backward upon the ground again, when something brought him bolt upright.

He rubbed his eyes, as if to clear them of some disturbing mist.

Had a star fallen and lay quivering, twinkling, sparkling in the little valley just at the foot of the mountains? For what was that dancing, glimmering point of light at the valley's edge?

Ah! there is another and another, and then they appear to be all about the valley just at the base of the mountains.

A long tongue of golden flame leaped up and settled the doubts and questions in Carroll's mind. God help us! the Indians have surrounded us with fire!

In an instant he had noiselessly awakened the men beside him No need of any words of explanation; they took in the situation at a glance, and, as if by instinct, they turned to Carroll.

"What is to be done, Carroll?"

"Well boys," he said quietly, " we must ride for our lives, and at once; it is certain death to stay here until daylight comes, provided we could do so; come on!"

Carroll rode a spirited, small bodied gray horse on his perilous journey, and the three men with him were as well mounted as himself.

Carroll flung a blanket over little Gray's head and with the rest following, their horses similarly hooded, led the way down to the western end of the valley. An immense fire had been kindled on each side of the narrow opening of the gorge, the light of one meeting the light of the other in a fierce yellow glow, all appearing as if arched, brazen gates barred the entrance to the gorge through which lay the way to safety.

Of course the central part of the valley was still wrapped in darkness, and under cover of its friendly shadow Carroll was enabled to lead little Gray almost down to the gorge.

It was a moment and a scene to test the courage of the man. He must plunge through that light and ride for life down through a narrow pass lined with skulking foes.

Carroll swung himself into the saddle, tore the blanket from his horses head, struck little Gray sharply with the spurs, and dropped low on the soft neck.

As swiftly, as if borne by a winged creature, Carroll was carried from the soft darkness into the ring of light.

Dazzled and blinded, he was borne beneath the great arch of flame, and then black shadows folded about him again as his horse's hoofs thundered down the hard bed of the gorge. He saw black forms crouch in astonished fear close to the rocky walls on either side, as this whirlwind flew by them, but danger and fire and savage foes shifted by like the phantom of a dream, and not until he drew rein in the wide western desert and looked back, did he realize the frightful peril he had escaped.

A flood of thankfulness filled his soul, and with it came a prayer for the safety of the comrades behind him.

Together they came, at a hard gallop, all unhurt, and as they caught up with Carroll, the terrible journey that they had begun, terrible from the fact that the four were utterly without food, the pack mules being left behind in their wild ride—seemed the thought uppermost in their minds. "Carroll," was the first question after they had joyfully greeted him—"Carroll, how are we going to get along until we get to Aurora?"

"Well boys, we will ride on until morning—it is growing a little lighter now—and then we'll stop and let the horses feed and rest a little, and then ride as fast as possible until our horses tire, when the same thing must be done over again, and yet again, until we reach food and Aurora."

The necessitous program thus concisely laid down was carried out in every detail. On the evening of the second day, with their belts tightened around them, as if to choke the fiend that was gnawing their vitals, and each man wondering, between paroxysms of hunger, if his face was as haggard and eyes as blood-shot as those of his neighbor, the little party staggered up a rocky gully in search of water.

They found it, and something else. "It's gold, boys," said Carroll, eying the glittering outcrop; "and if God permits us to reach Aurora we may all become rich men."

They were permitted to reach Aurora, and a week afterward, when somewhat recovered from the effect of his terrible journey, Carroll met and was introduced to the president of the Heintzelman mine, to whom Carroll made his report, the gentleman regarded him with amazement. "My dear sir," he exclaimed wonderingly, "I cannot imagine the reason for your being sent on such a perilous, needless errand; for Mr. Bradford knew at the time about the destruction of our works and the murder of its operatives. It surely was more than reprehensible in him."

"Where is Mr. Bradford?" inquired Carroll thoughtfully. "I cannot inform you, sir. He dissolved connection with the company last week, and his whereabouts are now unknown," answered the other.

Carroll courteously lifted his hat and turned away, but his heart was full of one thought in relation to Bradford, and that was: "Treachery." True to Carroll's prediction, the Golden Gulch, as it was named, was the source of a large fortune to its lucky finders.

Carroll, oppressed by a vague fear which he could not shake off, soon sold out, and with a millionaires fortune, started for the Eastern States.

A small, plain, little sitting room, whose bright fire shone on the faces of its occupants—a white faced, black robed woman, clasping a child in her arms, and a blonde bearded, hazel eyed man, whose face wore a look of well acted commiseration and sympathy toward one so nearly crushed by the evil tidings he had brought from the far west.

"Mrs. Carroll—Nettie," he said softly, "the burden laid on

those slender shoulders is too heavy for you to bear. Believe me to be thoroughly at your service, and——

"Owen Bradford!" thundered a voice that sounded like the trump of doom in the ears of the guilty man, "you have poured falsehoods enough into my wife's shrinking ears during the last six weeks. Take your accursed presence away from here, if you would not have me tear you limb from limb!"

As Owen Bradford went through the door, he saw Lionel Carroll catch his half fainting wife in his arms, saw the look of joy and love on her face as she threw her arms about his neck, then turning, he left the house, fully realizing that his dastardly scheme had failed, and only happiness and joy were the lot of the man whom he had sent through fire.

HANGED BY A GHOST.

In the year 1830 the confidential stewart of a wealthy settler near Sydney, Australia, stated that his master had suddenly been called to England on important business, and that during his absence the whole of his immense property would be his exclusive care. Some weeks after, an acquaintance of the absent settler riding through his grounds was astonished to see him sitting upon a stile. He strode forward to speak, when the figure turned from him with a look of intense sorrow and walked to the edge of a pond, where it mysteriously disappeared. On the morrow he brought a number of men to the water to drag it. And the body of the man supposed to be on his way to England was brought up. The stewart was arrested, brought to trial, and frightened at the story of his master's ghost, confessed the crime, stating that he did the murder at the very stile on which his master's ghost had appeared. He was duly executed.

"ARE YOU GOING TO KISS ME?"

If ever I go into a new locality again, says the correspondent of a Maine paper, I will study up my Geography better than I did this time, for my ignorance got me into a most uncomfortable position. As the boat neared Sanford I was standing with others on the deck when a very pretty young lady came up to me, and with a sweet smile on her face, looked into mine with a pair of lovely eyes, and asked, " Are you going to Kissme, sir?" If some one had offered to lend me ten dollars I could not have been more surprised, and scarcely knowing what to say, and in order to gain a little time, I gasped out: "Pardon, Miss, what did you ask?" I felt that she knew I heard her, but she said sweetly, "Are you going to Kissme to-night?" There was no misunderstanding her this time. I heard her and so did others, and I felt the blood rushing into my face, and I stammered out: "I would like to accommodate you Miss, I would, truly but I have a wife and thirteen children on board with me, and if my wife should see me kissing you"—"Kissing me! You hateful old thing! who asked you to kiss me?" "You did," I yelled; "you asked me twice!" "You old fool! I asked you if you were going to Kissme City to-night, don't you know anything?" and off she went, and if anybody felt meaner than I did, I would like to exchange photographs with him.

A FIGHT BETWEEN A DOG AND A SWAN.

People who were passing the large basin in one of the public gardens in Paris, recently saw a violent combat between the swan, whose abode was on this water, and a Spaniel whom thirst had attracted to the spot. The dog had approached the water and wished to quench his thirst. The swan thought it his duty to prevent the intruder from drinking at his water.

This contest had lasted about a quarter of an hour, when the dog, ashamed, as it seemed, of being thus beaten off by a bird, resolutely approached the brink, placed his two fore paws on the edge of the basin and with ears erect, and threatening teeth, defied the enemy. However a vigorous peck from the swan's bill sent him back bleeding on the grass. The Spaniel gets more angry and is determined to drink. He returns to the charge, dashing into the water, and swimming bravely up to the swan in his own element. The swan maintains his ground. The dog dashes into the water. Foolish animal! why did you not remain upon your own ground?

With two blows from his strong wings, the swan rolled him over in the shallow water where he lay bruised and half stunned. Then, with his long, flexible strong neck, the swan encircled the vanquished Spaniel, squeezed him and trampled on him so much that, had not a spectator come to the rescue, the dog would certainly have been killed.

This conflict proves that naturalists are right as to the great strength of the swan, when he chooses to display it.

A man from Columbus, Ohio, visited New York, went to church and seated himself without hesitation in the nearest pew. Soon the owner came in, eyed the stranger critically, and then writing "My Pew" on the fly leaf of a prayer book handed the book to the intruder. The Ohio man read the message, smole a beautiful smile, and wrote underneath, "nice pew, what do you pay for it?"

A cautious look around he stole,
His bag of chink he chunck,
And many a wicked smile he smole,
And many a wink he wunk.

If I was so unlucky as to have a stupid son, said an officer, I would certainly make him a parson. A clergyman who was in the company calmly replied, you think differently from your father.

Mr. Ebenezer Sweet was about to be joined in wedlock to Miss
Jane Lemon, when the editor of the local paper perpetrated the
following:

> How happy in extremes do meet
> Here Jane and Ebenezer;
> She is no longer sour, but sweet,
> And he's a lemon squeezer.

A JACK OF ALL TRADES.

Years ago, an English clergy man, hearing of a bishop of the
Episcopal Church of America, as famous alike for Godliness and
eloquence, went out of his way, during a tour in the United States,
to see him.

Coming to the town in which he resided, the traveler was
struck with the beauty of a Church that was nearly finished. Enter-
ing an opened door, he observed a group of work-men in the chan-
cel, and addressed one who seemed to be directing the others.
"Bishop Blank resides here, I believe?" "Yes." "Where is his palace?" "There," pointing to a plain brick dwelling across the street.

The Englishman was perplexed, being used to the pomps of
the Lord Bishop at home, who in their aprons and lawn sleeves
hold an imposing place in the House of Peers. "Ah! now, this
Church! very good indeed—pure style, better then I hoped to see in
America—who designed this stonework?" "I did" modestly replied
the man. "The master mason, eh! Who was your architect?" "I
was the architect too," said the man smiling. "Indeed! why, you
are Jack of all trades. You will tell me you designed the windows
next." "I did." The Englishman was amused. He chatted with
the workman a little, finding him to be singularly modest and
quiet in manner, but said at last, "I am going to pay my respects to
the Bishop. At what hour will I probably be admitted?" "You
will not find him at home now, I am the Bishop." Afterward the
Englishman in telling the story, said, I learned to know and
reverence him well after that; and I never knew a man so lacking
self-esteem. Whenever in the canticle, I thank God for the holy
and humble men of heart, I think of that American Bishop.

IN THEIR RIGHT PLACES.

The Brewers should to Malta go,
  The Boobies all to Scilly;
The Quakers to the friendly Isles,
  The Furriers to Chili;
The little darling caroling babes,
  That break our nightly rest,
Should be packed off to Baby-lon,
  To Lapland or to Brest.
From Spithead cooks go o'er to Greece,
  And while the miser waits
His passage to the Guinea Coast,
Spendthrifts are in the Straits.
  Let spinsters to the Needles go,
Wine bibbers to Burgundy;
  Send gourmands to the Sandwich Isles,
Wags to the Bay of Fun-dy;
  Bachelors to the United States,
Maids to the Isle of Man;
  Let gardeners go to Botany Bay,
And shoeblacks to Japan;
  Seek out all other misplaced men,
Lest they disturb and vex us,
  And all who're not provided for,
And send them off to Texas.

HE COULD HUG.

"Oh! will he bite," exclaimed one of Brooklyn's sweetest girls, with a look of alarm, when she saw one of the dancing bears in the street the other day, "No," said the escort, "he cannot bite, he is muzzled; but he can hug!" "Oh!" she said with a distracting smile, "I don't mind that."

EDWIN FORREST AND WHITE CLOUD.

Many years ago while Edwin Forrest was playing an engagement in a western theatre, White Cloud, and a number of other Indian chiefs were on their return from Washington. Stopping in the town over night they were conducted to the theatre to see the great American tragedian. Mr. Forrest was then in the prime of life. The play on that evening was Metamora. White Cloud and his band of warriors were accommodated with seats in a stage box. The theatre was crowded and it was evident that the audience were anxious to observe what effect the performance would have on the children of the forest. The play proceeded and although the Indians could not understand a word that was said, yet they appeared much interested, occasionally giving to one another a satisfactory grunt. After awhile they became rather uneasy.

This was more apparent when the Indian war whoop came from behind the scenes. The eyes of the audience were upon White Cloud, who two or three times grasped the tomahawk in his belt. The warriors did so likewise. The party were getting more excited as the play proceeded. They looked at each other with anxiety, their eyes indexed the fact that their souls were in arms. Presently Metamora, with uplifted tomahawk, rushed upon the stage, and when he gave the war whoop which none but a Forrest could give, the Indians could remain in their seats no longer. Forrest gave a second and a shriller whoop, whereupon White Cloud, and his band, joining in full chorus, sprang upon the stage, and brandishing their tomahawks and glittering knifes, rushed toward Metamora.

Forrest was dumbfounded for a moment, but he soon took in the situation, and, finding that the real Indians were on his side, ready to do, or die in his behalf, he felt that he had achieved one of his greatest triumphs in the profession he loved so well during his eventful life.

In detailing this ancedote Forrest said that he was not really aware at the time of the performance that he was using an exact whoop for reinforcements, but the wild Indians understood it, and responded as followers of Metamora.

The house was thrown into the wildest excitement, which soon cooled down with the general belief that it was the best performance and most effective rendition of the Indian play ever made by the distinguished actor.

MOTHER WIT.

One of Napoleon's veterans was wont to recount with great glee how he had once picked up the Emperor's hat at a review, when the Emperor, not noticing that he was a private, said carelessly: "Thank you, captain." "In what regiment, sir?" instantly asked the ready witted soldier.

Napoleon preceiving his mistake answered with a smile: "In my guard, for I see you know how to be prompt."

The newly made officer received his commission next morning.

A similar anecdote is related of Marshal Sonvoraff, who when receiving a dispatch from the hands of a Russian Sergeant who had distinguished himself on the Danube, tried to confuse the messenger by a series of whimsical questions, but found him equal to the occasion. How many fish are there in the sea? asked Sonvoraff.

All that are not caught yet, was the answer.

How far is it to the moon?

Two of your Excellency's forced marches.

What would you do if you saw your men giving way in battle?

I'd tell them there was a wagon load of whiskey just behind the enemies line.

The Marshal ended with: What's the difference between your Colonel and myself? My Colonel can not make me a lieutenant but your Excellency has only to say the word. I say it now, then, answered Sonvoraff, and a right good officer you'll be.

ROOM AND WORK FOR ALL.

Somewhere in some dusky corner
  Of the Poets busy brain,
With a ceaseless measured music,
  Beats an old and wise refrain.
Though a million eager claimants
  Crowd the ranks of duty's call,
Hold your chosen place undaunted—
  There is room and work for all!

If, amid the stress and tumult
  Of the surging conflict, Life,
Footsteps flag and hands grow weary
  Of the rude unequal strife;
If the strong, in selfish seeking,
  Crowd the weaker to the wall,
Hold your rightful place undaunted—
  There is room and work for all!

Oft the earnest striver, toiling,
  While the heavy load of care
Crushes heart and hope and courage
  To the black verge of despair;
Lifts again the irksome burden
  That her tired hands let fall,
Nerved anew by the assurance—
  There is room and work for all!

Ye who miss the chosen pathway,
  Still with patient diligence
Seek some field, however lowly—
  Earn a worthy recompense.
Do not fold your hands desponding,
  Lo! the writing on the wall
Was not meant for drones and idlers—
  There is room and work for all!

When you strive with earnest purpose,
  When you build with careful skill,
And the ruthless demon, failure,
  Thwarts your honest efforts, still
Try again, sincere endeavor
  Wins regard, however small;
While industry holds the balance,
  There is room and work for all!

"Luck" may set her place against you,
  Fickle fortune prove unkind;
But, howe'er the fates may use you
  Keep this maxim in your mind;
Till the heavens are rolled together,
  And the worlds foundations fall,
There is place for honest labor—
  There is room and work for all!

ODD BITS OF LIFE.

"C. Vanderbilt."

The man stood up in the municipal court as his name was called, says the Minneapolis Journal. He was a tramp. Just like any other tramp who is middle-aged, ragged, slouchy, and dirty. But he stood firmly, almost defiantly in the dock and looked the judge straight in the eye.

"Yer honor," said Officer Mulcahy, "I found the man wanderin' round the strate last night, an' he wouldn't give no account of his-self. He warn't drunk, but I run him in on gineral principles. He didn't have no valuables except a 'snipe' and this," and Officer Mulcahy laid the object on the table in front of the judge.

Only a baby's shoe!

Worn and frayed it was, with the buttons missing and the

lining torn. And yet there was an unusual quiet in the stuffy court room as the judge, with simulated sternness, looked down upon the prisoner and said: "Well what have you got to say for yourself?"

The tramp turned to the judge with an appealing look. His fingers twitched convulsively and his lip trembled as he said: "That shoe, judge, tells the whole story. It's my baby's shoe, and it's all I have in the world. Let me tell you my story. Five years ago I was prosperous and happy. I had a good trade and steady work. I had the nicest little wife in the world and the prettiest little baby girl that ever came into the world to make it brighter and better. Fool that I was I did not appreciate my blessings. I thought it was smart and manly to go out with the boys and drink my glass and stand treat with the rest of them. Sometimes I would come home drunk. My wife never complained, but there would be a look in her eye—oh, that I could tear it from my memory—and she grew pale and drooping, still uncomplaining.

"One night I came home drunk—'feeling good' as I used to call it. My wife came to the door to let me in. She said nothing, but the tears came to her eyes as she saw the condition I was in. That enraged me and I swore at her. The noise woke my little one and frightened her and she commenced to cry. Grasping her from her crib I tossed her high up to the ceiling, intending to catch her as she came down. I had forgotten that I was drunk, and I—I missed her. Down to the hard floor she fell with a crash and lay there without a motion, while the blood gushed from her nostrils. I had killed my child!

"My wife saw it all. From that moment she was a raving maniac. I stood horror-stricken and sobered for an instant, then rushed from the house. I never saw it again. I have become a wandering Jew; I feel the red-hot brand upon my brow. I can not stay in one place. I can not work. I can not sleep. Oftentimes have I been tempted to drown my sorrows with the flowing bowl, but that little shoe has kept me from drink. That's all I've got to say, judge: do with me as you will."

There was a suspicious moisture in the judge's eyes and Officer

Mulcahy was blowing his nose vigorously on his big bandana.

"You can go."

C. Vanderbilt made tracks for the door, not forgetting to take the little relic of his sorrowful tale. When he got outside the door he made a suspicious gesture with his thumb and finger and muttered to himself:

"I thought that yarn would fetch him. This 'ere shoe is meat and drink and liberty to me. Gets me anything I want. I'm glad the judge didn't ask me how I got the shoe when I left the house." And with a farewell flip of his fingers the tramp started for St. Paul.

A SWEDE WHO WOULD NOT ENGAGE IN A DUEL.

A correspondent of the Skenninge Posten relates an episode from Hanover in which a Swede played the principal part. It was at the technical high school in that city where engineer X. was pursuing some particular course of studies. Mr. X. was a giant in stature and possessed a giant's strength, but was so pious and docile that the German students had never seen his equal. He laughed at them when they engaged in duels. He laughed at them when they tried to vex him, and was in every way a very model of good nature. They tried to provoke him by asserting that he was a coward, in fact the greatest coward that had ever attended the high school. Mr. X. only laughed. And when his fellow students suggested that a sound threshing would cure him of his timidity, he laughed heartier than ever. But one day some one got it into his head to abuse Mr. X's nationality. Mr. X's looks become stern, and as soon as the effects of the new sally became apparent everybody commenced to shout in chorus that the Swedes were the most cowardly people in the world.

At this juncture Mr. X. issued a warning. That, however, had no effect. The students gathered about him and insisted that the Swedish kings were a set of faint hearted hares. Mr. X. selected the biggest one in the crowd and caused him to turn a few summer-saults in the room. That individual, amazed and blinded with rage gave X. a box on the ear, and then drew his sword. But now commenced a play which had not been looked for, and which is still fresh in the memory of many. Mr. X. whipped the whole crowd, about twenty in all—so severely that from that day the entire high school entertained the greatest respect for the Swedish giant, whose fists came near converting twenty students into sausage-meat. He was never afterward called a coward, and great deference was ever after shown the Swedish name, and the word" duel" was never again mentioned in his presence.

Mr. X., however, was good natured and laughed as before.

In former times, in the Scandinavian countries, the large wading birds, called storks, frequently built their nests on the straw-roofs of barns and other untenanted buildings. In this they were rather encouraged than otherwise, as the peasants considered it a very propitious omen to have storks nest on their premises, and consequently took particular pains to avoid frightening the birds away. On one occasion, Dr. H., of Aalborg, had a stork's nest on the roof of one of his out-houses, which for several years was occupied by the same pair of birds. One spring, however, the female stork arrived alone, but shortly afterwards a male bird appeared and the two soon agreed to remain with each other. They would go out and gather food, sometimes together, but more frequently separated and in different directions. Finally the female began to lay eggs and everything appeared to go on lovely. But one morning a terrible noise was heard to proceed from the stork's nest. Another male bird had arrived, this time the old mate of the female; he had come to take possession of his old home and family. A terrible fight ensued between the two male birds, so severe, indeed that the blood fairly flowed down the roof. After the battle the lately arrived male was seen to fly away, but he soon returned, accompanied by a large number of other storks, who pounced down upon the stork in possession of the nest, killed him and rolled his body down on the ground, whereupon the late-comer took charge of the nest and made himself at home as in days gone by.

Another incident relating to the peculiarities of these birds comes from Rev. N. in the village of S——. The minister's children had been out playing in the adjoining meadow and had there discovered a bird's nest with a large egg in it, round as a ball. The egg was taken home and shown to the minister, who became very indignant upon learning of his children's robbing a bird's nest. And as there was at the time no setting hen or duck on the premises, the minister ordered the hired man to crawl up on the barn-roof, and place the egg in a stork's nest which had been built there. The incident was soon forgotten; but one morning the storks were making an unusually loud noise over their nests, and they kept up the angry parleying for a long time, when suddenly the male bird flew away, apparently in a very ugly frame of mind. Soon he returned with four or five other storks, who also appeared very angry. These at once pounced upon the female bird and pecked her to death, where upon all the storks flew off together. Upon an examination being made of the nest it was found that a young owl had been hatched out from the round egg which had been placed there by the hired man, and that this little alien was the cause of the rage exhibited by the other storks. The mother bird had to pay with her life for her suspected perfidy.

ORIGIN OF BOCK BEER.

A HARROWING TALE OF A FEUDAL LORD, DARK BEER AND A GOAT.

The reputed origin of bock beer has been preserved in various legends which are current throughout Germany. At the town of Nuremberg, in the spring of a certain year during the feudal ages, an Easter Church fair was being held, which was participated in not only by the townsfolk but by people from all the countryside as well. There came riding into town a feudal Lord of great renown, who brought with him from Munich a quantity of light beer, which he praised very much. At the fair the people were drinking a dark beer, which the Lord looked upon with disdain.

After much discussion upon the relative merits of the light and dark beers a wager was laid, to be decided the following year when fair time should come around again. Each side was to brew a quantity of its favorite beer, and by a practical test it was to be ascertained how many mugs of each could be drank before making the drinker drunk. The beer that would make a man drunk first was to be awarded the palm.

At the next Easter fair the contestants sat down together in the presence of a vast concourse to decide the wager, the Lord drinking the dark-brown beer of the town and one cf the lustiest of the Nuremberger's drinking the Lord's light beer. A citizen kept tally of the number of mugs emptied by each. The Lord soon became hilarious and was finally exalted to a state of roaring intoxication long before his rival began to feel the effects of the light beer. Accordingly the dark beer was declared the winner of the contest and the townspeople sung the praises of their favorite beverage. While the people were still assembled a young goat, which is known in Germany as a buck or bock, broke into the space where the drinkers were sitting and rushing between the legs of the befuddled Lord threw him flat on his back, where, such was his condition, he was compelled to lie till he was picked up. From this circumstance comes the name of the dark-brown beer which still comes at Easter time.

Another legend is to the effect that the Jesuit monks were accustomed to hold a feast in the spring, at which they slaughtered a young goat or bock. To drink with this they brewed a dark, sweet beer which was considered a delicacy and which, when it became known outside of the monasteries, was hailed with delight by the people, and under the name of bock beer became an established institution.

When I first visited the now famous springs of Montana, distant three miles or less from Helena, though it was only thirteen years ago, I could not, by the widest stretch of fancy, have imagined that at this date one of the handsomest summer resort hotels on the continent would occupy the site of a coyote camp.

Yet the Hotel Broadwater is handsomer in finish, more complete in design and more beautiful in location than the best in five hundred of kindred resorts to the east and south. Why, just to think of porcelain bath tubs costing hundreds of dollars each in Chicago, of the two faucets in every room, one giving water at a temperature of 160 degrees, the other fluid as cold as the snow-caps covering the mountains which circle around this spot blessed by nature—water heated and cooled in the great receptacle of mother earth, remember. Then the big tank, with such a flow from the spring pipes that every one of 200 guests can be assured of 1,500 gallons to himself, though the whole 200 bathed at once. The hot water has a slightly sulphurous and not at all unpleasant taste, and careful analysis has shown that it almost exactly resembles in composition the waters of the famous springs in Arkansas. One spring shows traces of lithium, which will make it especially valuable for certain disorders.

THE EXPERIENCE OF THE OLD MAN IN A SWELL BARBER SHOP.

Any one could see by the old man's manner, as he entered the elegantly appointed city barber shop, that he was a little taken back by the splendor of the place. He hesitated just inside the door and glanced around in a bewildered way at the dazzling decorations, the marble floors, the rows of chairs and mirrors and white jacketed barbers, and when a porter took his valise and hat and hustled them away to the other side of the room his eyes followed them with an anxious and startled gaze, until he saw that they were properly cared for. Then he looked around and saw that half a dozen barbers had taken positions by as many vacant chairs and stood ready to tackle him.

"Where shall I set?" he asked.

"Take any chair, sir," said an attendant, and the old man got into the one nearest him and settled back with a solemn expression of countenance, as though he had begun to wonder what this thing was going to cost.

"Shave or hair cut?" asked the barber.

"Well, I did want both," answered the old man in a voice which might indicate that he was uncertain whether he still wanted both or not.

"All right, sir, I'll cut your hair first," and adjusting his chair the barber tucked cloths around the old man's neck and commenced operations.

"How'll you have it cut, sir?" he asked.

"Hey?"

"How'll you have it cut this time?"

"How?"

"Yes, want it short?"

"Wul, yes," answered the old man, as though it would have been a healthy idea to have it cut long.

"Neck shaved?" asked the barber, after he had been clipping for a while.

"Hey?

"Will you have your neck shaved?"

"Well, you're goin' ter shave my face, aint yer? I aint particular either way about my neck; shave it if yer wanter, though."

"Straight down, I suppose?"

"O, straight's yer can; I ain't perticular."

"Shampoo?" asked the barber a moment later.

"Hey?"

"Will you have a head wash?"

"Wul, I guess so; yes wash it out."

"Stand!" called the barber, and an assistant went over and placed a seat and towels beside the marble basin and then put a couple of eggs on a shelf in front of the barber's chair.

"Hard biled eggs for lunch?" asked the old man, who had begun to feel a little more at home.

"No," answered the barber; "those are raw eggs for the shampoo."

"Does he eat 'em raw?"

"Who?"

"The shampoo."

The gentlemanly barber explained that the eggs were for the head wash; that they were very much better than the prepared stuff for that purpose; made the hair nice and soft, and had no bad effect on the scalp. Then he took one of the eggs, tapped it gently on the corner of the shelf, picked a little hole in the end of it and began to pour out the contents slowly on the old man's head.

"Hold on there! Hold on!" exclaimed the old gentleman excitedly, sitting up straight. "I guess this thing's gone 'bout fur enough now. It's all right ter be askin' me fool questions about whether I want m' hair cut short er long, 'n' whether I want m' neck shaved 'n' m' head washed. It's all right ter try an' make a fool of an old man in that way ef yer wanter, but by gosh! ef yer think you're goin' ter send me out o'here 'th m' hair all stuck up with aig—How much do I owe yer?" he asked, standing up and trying to pull the cloths from around his neck.

The proprietor of the shop labored a long time to convince the old man that they had not been making game of him, but it was not until a good natured customer in one of the chairs ordered an egg shampoo and allowed the eggs to be poured into his hair that the old gentleman became satisfied. Then he meekly climbed back into the chair and told the barber to go ahead.

The barber rubbed and rubbed and worked up a lather, led the old man like a lamb over to the basin, squirted hot and cold water over his head and into his ears, led him back to the chair, shaved him, spatted him with wet towels, molded and kneaded his face, dug out his ears, oiled his hair and combed it barber style; and through it all the old man never opened his mouth or uttered a sound; but when the boy had slapped him all over with a whisk broom, and he had paid his bill of nintey cents and walked solemnly out, it was apparent that he was doing a heap of thinking.

A CUTE DEAD-HEAD.

San Francisco Examiner: "Talking about free passes," said Mart Henley, who is the manager of Ned Harrigan, "I was once worked in the cutest way imaginable. A fellow came to me and represented that he was the dramatic, critic of a leading newspaper. I was sure he did not tell the truth, and to get rid of him said the paper had been abusing our show, and could not get any passes.

"'Oh, that is all right,' he replied, I've been away. I'll fix that and give you a good send-off.'"

"The next day he came to me with a copy of the paper containing a fine puff for our show. I looked the article over and gave him a box. When I told Ned of it he said: "'That's funny. I saw the paper to-day and it roasted us.'

"I told Ned he was mistaken, and we made a bet on it. I got the paper the fellow had left me, and there was the article. Ned got another copy of the paper, and the roasting it gave us was awful. How did it happen? Well, the fellow was a printer on the paper. He had set up a puff, taken proof of it, and pasted it so neatly over the abusive article that I did not detect it at first."

www.ingramcontent.com/pod-product-compliance
Lightning Source LLC
Chambersburg PA
CBHW021409090426

42742CB00009B/1072